Arroyo Center

MILITARY EXPENDITURES AND ECONOMIC GROWTH

Jasen Castillo, Julia Lowell, Ashley J. Tellis, Jorge Muñoz, Benjamin Zycher

RAND

Prepared for the
United States Army

Approved for public release; distribution unlimited

The research described in this report was sponsored by the United States Army under Contract No. DASW01-96-C-0004.

Library of Congress Cataloging-in-Publication Data

Military expenditures and economic growth / Jasen Castillo ... [et al.].
p. cm.
"MR-1112-A."
Includes bibliographical references.
ISBN 0-8330-2896-0
1. Armed Forces—Appropriations and expenditures. 2. Economic development. 3. Gross domestic product. 4. Great powers—History—19th century. 5. Great powers—History—20th century. I. Castillo, Jasen

UA17 .M554 2001
355.6'229—dc21

00-062667

Published 2001 by RAND
1700 Main Street, P.O. Box 2138, Santa Monica, CA 90407-2138
1200 South Hayes Street, Arlington, VA 22202-5050
RAND URL: http://www.rand.org/
To order RAND documents or to obtain additional information, contact Distribution Services: Telephone: (310) 451-7002;
Fax: (310) 451-6915; Internet: order@rand.org

PREFACE

This report presents an exploration of the historical relationship between national economic growth and military expenditures in five "great power" countries: Germany, France, Russia, Japan, and the United States. Using statistical as well as case study methodologies, it examines how each country's military expenditures responded to increases in output levels and rates of growth over the period 1870–1939 and proposes plausible explanations for the relationship in each country. If the historical experience holds true, economic growth in some of the present-day candidates for great-power status will spur them to increase their rate of military expenditure growth and, as a result, their military capabilities. As we show, however, each country is unique, and strong economic growth by no means implies automatic expansion of military spending or capabilities. In fact, the historical record suggests that perceived threats from abroad may be the most significant factor contributing to increases in military expenditure in potential great powers. This distinction is important because policies designed to deter foreign military expansions motivated by ambition may have perverse effects if foreign military expansions are in fact motivated by fear.

This report should be of particular interest to policymakers concerned about the prospect of increased military expenditures by large and rapidly growing economies. The research was sponsored by the Deputy Chief of Staff for Intelligence and was conducted in RAND Arroyo Center's Strategy, Doctrine, and Resources Program. The Arroyo Center is a federally funded research and development center sponsored by the United States Army.

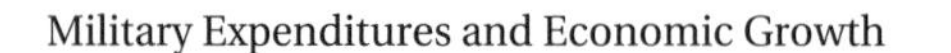

For more information on RAND Arroyo Center, contact the Director of Operations (tel 310-393-0411, extension 6500; FAX 310-451-6952; e-mail donnab@rand.org), or visit the Arroyo Center's Web site at http://www.rand.org/organization/ard/

CONTENTS

FIGURES

TABLES

SUMMARY

By increasing their military expenditures, states with rapidly industrializing economies have the potential to develop significant military capabilities. Whether or not they choose to do so is of considerable policy relevance to the United States. In this monograph report, we look at the relationship between military expenditures and economic growth in five "great power" states—Germany, France, Russia, Japan, and the United States—each of which experienced rapid economic growth and industrialization in the decades following 1870. We choose these states for our examination because their military spending choices may provide useful insights into the choices of other potential powers that are either on the cusp of, or already undergoing, a similar economic takeoff.

In the report, we address the following research questions:

1. To what extent did movements in military expenditures match movements in output levels and rates of growth in each of the relevant countries during the period 1870–1939?
2. What are the most plausible explanations for the increases in military expenditures that took place in each country?

Our approach to the first question consists of a descriptive data analysis together with statistical tests of the military expenditures–output relationship. We find that, for France, Germany, and the United States, none devoted a dramatically increasing share of their growing national resources to their militaries as they experienced profound economic transformations in nonwar years between 1870 and 1913. The share of Japanese output devoted to military expenditures, in contrast, more than doubled over the same period. In the tumultuous period between the two world wars, military expenditures in all countries except the United States shot up dramatically. This occurred despite the global economic recession that prevailed during the first part of the period.

In statistical terms, for any given country during any given year in the sample period, the best predictor of military expenditures is the level of military expenditures in the previous year. The statistical evidence does not support generalizations about a positive relationship between output levels or output growth and military expenditures. This is still the case when we allow for lags of several years between changes in output and military spending decisions. Further, other measures we use to proxy for other factors that might influence military decisionmakers—such as the number of military personnel in rival states—also do not appear to be consistently related to changes in military expenditures over time.

Thus, the states in our sample appear to have made their military spending decisions in response to changes in political and economic circumstances that are not adequately captured by the measures available to us. Given the limits imposed on statistical models by the historical data, a case study approach may offer a richer menu of possible explanations for the military expenditures that took place in each country. To address the second question, therefore, we conduct historical case studies of the five great powers, sorting our 1870–1940 sample into three time periods: Post-Bismarck, 1870–1890; pre–World War I, 1890–1913; and pre–World War II, 1919–1939. We propose three alternative hypotheses to explain the pattern of military expenditures we observe.

The first of our alternatives, the "ambition" hypothesis, posits that states experiencing economic growth develop foreign policy ambitions that motivate them to increase their military expenditures. The second alternative, the "fear" hypothesis, argues that states increase their military spending when they perceive heightened threats to their security. The third alternative, the "legitimacy" hypothesis, argues that governments faced with domestic threats to their political legitimacy increase their military spending in support of aggressive foreign policies that garner support at home. Of the three, only the ambition hypothesis suggests that economic growth is in itself a sufficient condition for increasing the share of resources devoted to military spending.

Our results are summarized in Table S.1. We find some support for all three hypotheses, but the fear hypothesis most consistently appears to explain the historical record. In fact, we believe that fear was a driving factor behind accelerating military spending in 12 out of 15 of the historical episodes we examine. In contrast, we find relatively little evidence for the legitimacy hypothesis: although domestic politics certainly played some role in all of the foreign policy and procurement decisions we examine, only two episodes (Germany, 1891–1913, and Japan, 1919–1939) seem to exhibit the dynamics associated with securing domestic political legitimacy.

Economic growth through modernization seems to have been key to achieving ambitious foreign policies for certain states at certain times—e.g., France, Russia, and the United States in 1870–1890 and Germany, Japan, Russia, and the United States in 1891–1913—but in the later periods ambition is always accompanied by fear. This observation is important because policies that might be successful at deterring foreign military expansions motivated by aggression might have the opposite effect if such expansions are motivated by fear. In the modern context, this means that U.S. attempts to counter the perceived military ambitions of a newly rising power through force modernization and expansion in some cases have the potential to trigger an arms race.

Table S.1

Which Hypotheses Explain Great-Power Military Spending?

Period	France	Germany	Japan	Russia	United States
1870–1890	Ambition	Fear	Fear	Ambition	Ambition
1891–1913	Fear	Ambition, fear, and legitimacy	Ambition and fear	Ambition and fear	Ambition and fear
1919–1939	Fear	Ambition and fear	Ambition, fear and legitimacy	Fear	Fear

To understand fully why the five great powers we examine did or did not increase their militaries' share of national resources requires a finer-grained analysis than has been carried out in this study. However, their motives probably included complex combinations of ambition, fear, and, to a lesser extent, legitimacy. Unfortunately, a quantitative examination of the exact mix of these motives for these five countries is outside the scope of this report because of, among other factors, the paucity of good and detailed historical data. However, for extensions of the analysis to would-be great powers of today, such data may well be available, offering the potential for a more considered response based on deeper judgments about why any individual country's military expenditures are growing and how they are being allocated. In the last chapter of the report, we identify variables that, constructed from adequate data, would allow us to better discriminate among the three hypotheses.

Chapter One

DEFINING THE PROBLEM

Whether states choose to accelerate their military expenditures in response to widespread industrialization and rapid domestic economic growth is a question of considerable policy relevance to the United States.[1] If the relationship obtains, states with rapidly industrializing economies are likely also to develop significant military capabilities. But the extent to which this relationship should concern U.S. policymakers, if it obtains, depends on at least two additional factors: the potential economic size and strategic importance of the state (could it become a "great power"?) and the motives behind its military buildup.

Size is important because big states have immediate command over more resources than small states. Geography is important because strategically placed states have the potential to extort concessions from other states. These characteristics make big or strategic states inherently worth watching. Motives are also important, in part because U.S. actions based on a misreading of motives could trigger an increasingly belligerent and adversarial relationship, damaging to all parties. For example, an aggressive arms buildup by any state, particularly a big one, might warrant a U.S. counterresponse. But an overreactive U.S. response to what is a purely defensive arms buildup

[1]The terms "national output," "economic output," and "output" are used interchangeably throughout the report, while the term "growth" is often substituted for the term "output growth." "Military expenditures" and "military spending" are also used interchangeably throughout. Alternative measures of these concepts are introduced and discussed in Chapter Three.

might be counterproductive, reinforcing the fear that sparked the buildup in the first place.

We examine whether five historic great powers—Germany, France, Russia, Japan, and the United States—undertook dramatic increases in their military spending on entering their "takeoff" period of rapid economic growth and industrialization.[2] We choose these states because their behavior may provide useful insights into the behavior of other potential powers either on the cusp of, or already undergoing, a similar economic takeoff. (A sixth power, the United Kingdom, is not included because its takeoff period occurred considerably before the others.[3]) Formally, we set out to answer the following research questions:

1. To what extent did movements in military expenditures match movements in output levels and rates of growth in each of the relevant countries during the period 1870–1939?
2. What are the most plausible explanations for the increases in military expenditures that took place in each country?

Although there is an extensive economics and international relations literature on the relationship between economic growth and increased military expenditures, it does not adequately establish answers to these two questions. One reason is that most empirical studies set economic growth as the independent variable, focusing on the effects of military expenditures on economic growth rather than the other way around. A second reason is that we found no studies that look at the military expenditures–growth relationship in the context of the historical experience of great powers. We believe that this context is important for the reasons stated above.

---

[2]The concept of takeoff, made prominent by W. W. Rostow's celebrated 1960 volume, *The Stages of Economic Growth*, refers to a period in which nations experience dramatic economic transformation that manifests itself through growth rates far greater than the historical norm as well as critical alterations in the structure of the national economy.

[3]Although its economic take-off happened before the modernization of the great powers we examine here, future research should consider adding the British Empire, since its geography, and therefore its strategic position, mirrors the United States in many ways. Italy and the Austro-Hungarian Empire are different matters. We exclude them from the analysis because their capabilities fell far short of the other great powers we examine over the nearly 70-year period.

Admittedly the difficulties of obtaining adequate data for such a study are daunting, and we have by no means surmounted them all. Nevertheless, we feel that even imperfect data are worth exploiting if they can clarify these important questions. We would like this report to be viewed as an effort at organizing limited, patchy, and disparate data in a way that allows us to explore a problem of great interest to policymakers.

In this report, we address question 1 in quantitative terms. We provide empirical estimates of the sign but not magnitude of the relationship between military spending, output, and output growth. Question 2 is addressed exclusively in qualitative terms not only because we lack the quantitative data required to discriminate among alternative hypotheses, but also because alternative hypotheses must be generated within a historical context. However, the alternative hypotheses that we propose are elaborated in some detail, and the data requirements for discriminating among them are identified. By so doing we provide a set of indicator variables we hope will be useful to policymakers when analyzing economic and military trends in newly rising powers.

This report is organized as follows: Chapter Two surveys the existing literature for findings about the relationship between economic growth and military spending. Chapter Three presents our empirical findings on the historical relationship between military expenditures and growth for Germany, France, Russia, Japan, and the United States. Chapter Four outlines alternative hypotheses about the military expenditures–growth relationship and identifies indicator variables. Chapter Five presents qualitative historical evidence on the alternative hypotheses. Chapter Six offers thoughts on whether the United States ought to worry about large, fast-growing economies in light of the historical record.

While this report should be of interest to the intelligence community, the Department of Defense, and U.S. policymakers as a whole, it should also be of value to academics and scholars interested in the relationship between economic growth and military power.

Chapter Two

A BRIEF REVIEW OF THE STATISTICAL LITERATURE

The major strand of the literature on the statistical relationship between military spending and economic growth comes from the field of development economics, where a host of studies have attempted to determine the influence of defense expenditures on economic development. According to the conventional wisdom—which is encapsulated in the official policy of lending institutions such as the World Bank and International Monetary Fund (IMF)—government expenditures on national defense carry an opportunity cost in the form of lower economic output and slower rates of output growth.[1] The theoretical assumption is that resources spent on preparation for war, and on warfighting itself, could be better employed elsewhere. In particular, the devotion of valuable human capital to military rather than civilian research and development is assumed to significantly retard economic growth. Thus, a popular assumption for researchers and policymakers alike is that the influence of military spending on economic growth is negative.

But the empirical evidence on the military expenditures–growth relationship is decidedly ambiguous. In a study of 44 developing economies, for example, Benoit (1973) found no evidence that defense spending has an adverse effect on growth. In fact, even after controlling for reductions in foreign investment and aid as a result of military spending, the correlation between military expenditures and economic growth remained positive. More recently, a study by Babin (1986) looked at 88 developing economies from 1965 to 1981.

[1] See, for example, Nelson (1963), Benoit (1968), and Knight et al. (1996).

Babin also found a consistently positive relationship and concluded that military stability—which requires military capability—is an important precondition for economic advancement in the Third World.[2]

A second and much smaller strand of the literature explicitly considers the impact of economic growth on military expenditures. One example is Looney (1994), where data from 1965 to 1987 are used to construct a system of equations that allow for the relative influence of resource availability, trade patterns, indigenous arms production, and other political and strategic, as well as economic, variables. For arms producers as well as nonproducers, the model suggests that economic production has a significant positive influence on defense spending.

Still a third strand of the literature uses purely statistical, or "atheoretical" techniques to determine the relationship between military spending and growth. Smith (1989) takes an iterative approach to modeling the relationship, setting up alternatives and then using a series of specification tests to determine which alternatives best fit the data. In an examination of British military expenditures post-1945, Smith found that military expenditures are a positive function of economic performance and the relative price of military and nonmilitary goods, as well as security variables based on threat appreciation and military alliances. In a test of the model's applicability to other countries, Smith found it also fit data for France.

Chowdhury (1991) and Kusi (1994) each conducted tests of the direction of statistical causality between military expenditures and growth. A summary of their findings is presented in Table 2.1. In both studies, the results suggest that the relationship between defense spending and economic growth cannot be generalized across countries. However, where a relationship does appear to exist, there is slightly more evidence to suggest that increases in military expenditures anticipate declines in economic growth, while increases in economic growth anticipate increases in military expenditures.[3]

---

[2]This conclusion is consistent with arguments presented in Wolf (1981).

[3]The results of these studies are susceptible to the problems associated with Granger's (1969) causality estimation, namely the potential bias of the estimators because of inappropriate lag estimation, and the problems associated with errors in the source

Table 2.1

Comparison of Causality Results, Chowdhury (1991) and Kusi (1994)

Sample and Findings	Chowdhury	Kusi
Number of countries	55	77
Number (percent) of countries with result:		
No statistically significant causal relationship	30 (55)	62 (80)
Military expenditures reduced economic growth	15 (27)	3 (4)
Military expenditures increased economic growth	0	4 (5)
Economic growth reduced military expenditures	1 (2)	1 (1)
Economic growth increased military expenditures	9 (16)	6 (8)

Finally, a fourth strand of the literature traces its approach to the seminal model of an arms race developed by Richardson (1960). In Richardson-type models, arms acquisitions are described in terms of simultaneous linear reaction functions, where states change their levels of military expenditure in response to the level of military expenditure in rival states. A recent model of this type is Looney (1990), in which the causal factors behind the arms races in the Middle East are explored. Applying a Hsiao test to different pairs of countries, Looney identifies the sequence of steps that contribute to each bilateral arms race.[4] Looney identifies four possible cases:

1. Defense (A) causes defense (B)
2. Defense (B) causes defense (A)
3. Joint causality between (A) and (B)
4. No relationship.

One of the most interesting of Looney's findings is that country A may affect arms expenditures in country B even when country B does not affect country A. Another interesting finding is that the defense expenditure of an ally can spark the same increase as the defense expenditure of an adversary, with an even shorter lag.

data, which Johansen (1988) discusses. Granger (1988) also points out that if military expenditure is adjusted optimally to keep output at determined target levels given exogenous shocks, there may be no observable correlation.

[4]A description of the test can be found in Hsiao (1979).

Unfortunately, the variables included in the Looney approach are limited to defense expenditures, so that such factors as resource availability or economic growth are ignored. Arms race models that incorporate economic aspects in their formulation are more interesting for our purposes. The model presented by Wolfson and Shabahang (1991), for example, addresses the question, "What patterns of economic development will cause an acceleration of an arms race and increase the dangers of war?" Wolfson and Shabahang construct a model of international economic-military equilibrium and then subject it to destabilizing economic growth patterns. Because it allows researchers to address the issue of asymmetric economic growth patterns between adversaries, their model is richer than those that employ simple defense expenditure reaction equations. Tested against the experience of the Anglo-German arms race prior to World War I, their model confirms the widely held belief that rapid growth, a high level of savings, and rapid technological progress in Germany prior to World War I prompted Britain to devote increased resources to defense right up until the two countries declared war on each other in 1914.

CONCLUSION

An important lesson from the statistical literature on the military expenditures–growth relationship is that it is difficult to generalize empirically across countries. A number of country- and time-specific variables can influence how much a state decides to spend on defense. In addition, problems of data availability and measurement contribute to the difficulty of identifying generic patterns, particularly where developing countries are concerned. Some of the empirical differences between models, therefore, may be simply explained by differences in researchers' choice of time period, country grouping, data averaging methodology, and level of data aggregation.

Further, although some models incorporate such political variables as the type of government regime and social structure, other politico-economic, sociocultural, and historical characteristics may influence the relationship between military spending and economic growth and are more difficult to capture. For some states, for example, the ability to provide a credible national defense may substitute for the procurement of other social needs as the root of national support and legitimacy. For others, a history of external conflicts stemming from geostrategic, ideological, religious, ethnic, or other considerations may cause them to place a priority on defense that is very hard to accommodate in statistical models.

Ideally, we would like to have been able to include the various economic, politico-economic, and sociocultural explanatory variables that theory suggests belong in a formal empirical model of the determinants of great-power military spending. Unfortunately, for the time period we are considering, at best only rudimentary economic and political data are available. Therefore, we ask instead two much simpler questions. First, how much of the variation in national military expenditures over time appears to be explained by movements in national output? Second, what is the direction of influence? Our results, and the caveats that attend them, are reported in the next chapter.

Chapter Three

EMPIRICAL DETERMINATION OF THE GROWTH–MILITARY EXPENDITURES RELATIONSHIP

We begin our empirical analysis with a simple comparison of trends for each of the "great power" countries from approximately 1870 to 1939. Simple graphs show how such historical events as the Russo-Japanese War or the Versailles Treaty influenced movements in military expenditures and economic output. They also provide an initial test of the universality of the military expenditures–growth relationship without being subject to the data requirements of a more formal statistical analysis.

To control for some of the other factors that may influence domestic resource allocation toward the military, however, statistical analysis is a useful tool. In particular, a system of regressions explicitly allows for the possibility that increases in one country's military expenditures, or in the size of its armed forces, might influence another country's decision on how much to spend. We stress, however, that our analysis here asks simply whether the relationships illustrated in the graphs appear robust when other variables are factored in. Our focus is on the sign rather than the magnitude of particular parameters because data limitations—including significant numbers of missing observations—preclude more precise estimation.

DATA DESCRIPTION

Our data consist of annual measures of national output, military expenditures, military personnel, and government expenditures for each country, plus price deflators and currency exchange rates for making cross-national comparisons. Measures of real output growth are calculated by taking the log difference of real output. An index measuring the general openness of political institutions is also employed. The sample period is 1870 to 1939. A primary reason for our choice of a particular data source was because of the availability of an extended and reasonably representative time series. Nevertheless, for some countries and some variables data are incomplete, as described in Tables 3.1 through 3.5 below.

National Output Measures

For France, we considered two alternative inflation-adjusted (real) output measures: a real Gross Domestic Product (GDP) series based on average prices in France over the period 1905–1913 (in francs), and a nominal GDP series converted to 1982 U.S. dollars using exchange rates from Mitchell (1988) and a U.S. implicit price deflator from Romer (1989). A U.S., rather than French, price deflator was used to construct the second real output series to allow for consistent comparisons with data for which appropriate national deflators are not available.[1] No French output or price data are available for the period 1914–1919. For reasons of cross-national comparability, the second measure is used and described here.

For Germany, again two alternative inflation-adjusted output measures are considered: a real Net National Product (NNP) series reflecting average prices in German marks in 1913, and a nominal GDP series converted to 1982 dollars using exchange rates and an implicit price deflator obtained from the sources described above. No German output or price data are available for the period 1914–1924. Again, the second measure is used for the reasons given above.

For Japan, one output measure we considered was real Gross National Product (GNP), a series constructed by Ohkawa, Takamatsu, and Yamamoto (JSA, 1987) and measured in 1936–1938 yen. A second measure was Productive National Income (PNI), a series constructed by Yamada (JSA, 1987) on the basis of historical estimates of national productive capacity. This last, longer, series is used here and converted to dollars using exchange rates from JSA (1987, Vol. 3).

---

[1]Although the use of a domestic deflator would have been preferable, large gaps in the domestic data precluded this option.

It is adjusted to reflect 1982 prices with the deflator provided in Romer (1989).

No broad measure of national economic output is available for Russia during the time period of interest. Accordingly, to explore how Russian military spending responded to increases in the size of Russia's economy we considered two proxies: Russian domestic production of iron and steel, measured in tons, and Russian energy consumption, measured in coal-ton equivalents. Table 3.1 shows the simple correlations between real output and the energy and iron and steel variables for the other four nations. All the correlations are highly positive; this suggests that both energy consumption and iron and steel production are good instruments with which to substitute for the unavailable Russian real output data. The simple correlation between the two instruments is also high at 0.985; to keep things simple, therefore, we report here only the regression results for iron and steel.

Finally, for the United States, real output in 1982 dollars is taken from Romer (1989). A summary of information on the national output measures for all five countries in our sample is presented in Table 3.2.

Table 3.1

Output Correlations with Coal Consumption and Iron/Steel Production

	GDP			
	U.S.	France	Germany	Japan
Energy	0.99			
Iron and steel	0.94			
Energy		0.70		
Iron and steel		0.56		
Energy			0.86	
Iron and steel			0.90	
Energy				0.88
Iron and steel				0.69

Table 3.2

National Output Measures: Five Great Powers, 1870–1939

Country	Measure	Units	Data Availability	Source[a]
France	Real GDP (1)	1905–1913 francs, millions	1870–1913, 1920–1938	Mitchell (1992, J1)
	Real GDP (2)	1982 dollars, millions	1870–1913, 1920–1938	Mitchell (1992, J1); Mitchell (1988); Romer (1989)
Germany	Real NNP	1913 marks, millions	1870–1913, 1925–1938	Mitchell (1992), J1)
	Real GDP	1982 dollars, millions	1873–1913, 1925–1939	Mitchell (1992, J1); Mitchell (1988); Romer (1989)
Japan	Real GNP	1936–1938 yen, millions	1885–1939	JSA (1987)
	Real PNI	1982 dollars, millions	1875–1939	JSA (1987); Romer (1989)
Russia	Iron and steel production	Thousand tons	1870–1939	Singer and Small (1993)
	Energy consumption	Thousand coal-ton equivalents	1870–1939	Singer and Small (1993)
United States	Real GNP	1982 dollars, millions	1870–1939	Romer (1989)

[a]Table number follows publication year where relevant.

Military Expenditure Measures

As pointed out by Herrmann (1996, Appendix B), official statistical publications often understate the true magnitude of military spending because governments routinely try to conceal important elements of their military expenditures. Different official and scholarly publications therefore report varying military spending estimates depending on their criteria for inclusion and the purpose for which the data are to be used. Although we choose our series to be as closely comparable as possible in their treatment of various categories of military expenditures, significant differences may exist. An exhaustive comparison of the data collection methodologies for these series was beyond the scope of this study.

We obtained data on military expenditures for France, Germany, and Russia from Singer and Small (1993). As this source expresses data for 1870–1913 in British pounds and data for 1914–1939 in dollars, each series was converted to dollars using exchange rates from Mitchell (1988). Data for Japan were obtained from JSA (1987) and converted to dollars using exchange rates obtained from the same source. Data for the United States were obtained from Census (1975). For all countries, inflation-adjusted measures were calculated using the deflator in Romer (1989). The data and other sources are summarized in Table 3.3.

Table 3.3

Real Military Expenditures: Five Great Powers, 1870–1939

Country	Units	Data Availability	Source
France	1982 dollars, millions	1870–1939	Singer and Small (1994); Mitchell (1988); Romer (1989)
Germany	1982 dollars, millions	1870–1939	Singer and Small (1993); Mitchell (1988); Romer (1989)
Japan	1982 dollars, millions	1870–1939	Singer and Small (1993); Mitchell (1988); Romer (1989)
Russia	1982 dollars, millions	1870–1939	Singer and Small (1993); Mitchell (1988); Romer (1989)
United States	1982 dollars, millions	1870–1939	Singer and Small (1993); Romer (1989)

Military Personnel Measures

Data on military personnel serve not only to confirm or contest patterns suggested by data on military expenditures, but also provide one reasonable proxy for the military threat to each of our five great-power countries.[2] For France prior to 1918, we calculate a "threat" variable consisting of the sum of German and Austro-Hungarian military personnel; after 1918 it is just German military personnel.

[2]A second proxy is military spending in friendly as well as rival states; the two different approaches are discussed more fully in the estimation section below.

For Germany, the threat is the sum of Russian, French, and English military personnel; for Japan, it is the sum of Russian and U.S. military personnel; for Russia, it is the sum of Japanese, German, and, prior to 1918, Austro-Hungarian military personnel; and for the United States, it is Japanese and German military personnel.

However, as discussed at length in Herrmann (1996, Appendix A), the various statistical publications of the great-power governments used quite divergent criteria for computing the number of officers and men under arms. Thus, only a very general sense of the relative strength of each country's military can be obtained from these data.[3] As shown in a limited way in the figures below, the data we use are on the whole consistent with other published sources.

For France, Germany, and the United States, the military personnel data count active-duty army and navy personnel only. For Japan, data from 1899 on include civilian employees of the Japanese Army as well as active-duty army and navy officers and men. For Russia, only one data source is available and the breakdown is not clear: In 1916–1917, for example, the number presented may include civilians connected to the war effort. Coverage details are given in Table 3.4.

Government Expenditure Measures

Two plausible alternative measures of a nation's fear of—or desire for—war are, first, military spending as a proportion of national output and, second, military spending as a proportion of government expenditures. Generally speaking, the larger the role played by the government in the economy, the closer the two measures will be. It can be argued that military spending as a share of government expenditures is most useful as a measure of warlike intent, while military spending as a proportion of national output is most useful as a measure of military capability.

The measure of government expenditures available to us is central government expenditures (CGE), which does not include local- and state-level resource allocations. While this works well for countries

---

[3]The figures for 1914–1918 are particularly unreliable as several governments ceased publishing comparative statistics when the war broke out.

Table 3.4

Military Personnel: Five Great Powers, 1870–1939

Country	Units	Data Availability	Source[a]
Austria-Hungary	Thousands of active-duty personnel	1870–1913, 1919–1938	Flora (1987, Ch. 6)
France	Thousands of active-duty personnel	1870–1913, 1919–1938	Flora (1987, Ch. 6)
Germany	Thousands of active-duty personnel	1870–1913, 1919–1938	Flora (1987, Ch. 6)
Japan	Thousands of personnel	1876–1935; 1937–1939	JSA (1987, 26-3-a)
Russia	Thousands of personnel	1870–1939	Singer and Small (1993)
United States	Thousands of active-duty personnel	1870–1939	Census (1975, Y 904–916)

[a]Table number follows publication year where relevant.

such as France, where the administration is highly centralized, it is more problematic for countries such as Germany or the United States that have federal political structures. And because of differences in definition, the series are not comparable across countries: For example, the German data include expenditures on social insurance institutions, while the U.S. data include interest payments on the public debt. There are also many missing observations. For the purposes of this analysis, therefore, we track military expenditures-to-CGE only as a measure of changes in military posture within a single country over time. Table 3.5 gives coverage details.

Political Participation Measure

Finally, according to some political theorists, the more accessible a country's political institutions are, the less likely it is to pursue aggressive foreign policies. We use an index of political participation constructed by Gurr, Jaggers, and Moore (GJM) (1990) as one of the

Table 3.5

Central Government Expenditures: Five Great Powers, 1870–1939

Country	Measure	Units	Data Availability	Source[a]
France	CGE	New franc, millions	1870–1939	Mitchell (1992)
Germany	CGE	Mark, millions	1872–1921; 1924–1934	Mitchell (1992)
Japan	CGE	Yen, millions	1870–1939	JSA (1987)
Russia	CGE	Paper rubles, millions	1870–1914; 1924–1934; 1938	Mitchell (1992)
United States	Central government outlays[b]	Dollar, thousands	1870–1939	Census (1975, Y 904–916)

[a]Table number follows publication year where relevant.

[b]At the aggregate central government level, outlays and actual expenditures are approximately equal.

explanatory variables in our statistical analysis. In the GJM system, a 10 indicates that national political institution are very open (democracy), a 0 indicates that they are closed (autocracy). Average index values for each country using the GJM system are presented in Table 3.6.

Table 3.6

Political Participation Indexes: 1870–1939 Averages

Country	1870–1880	1881–1890	1891–1900	1901–1913	1914–1919	1920–1932	1933–1939
France	5.7	7.0	7.3	8.0	8.0	9.2	10.0
Germany	0.7	1.3	4.0	4.5	5.2	6.0	0.0
Japan	5.0	5.0	5.0	5.0	5.0	5.0	5.0
Russia	0.0	0.0	0.0	1.0	1.7	0.2	0.0
United States	9.9	10.0	10.0	10.0	10.0	10.0	10.0

SOURCE: Gurr, Jaggers, and Moore (1990).

TRENDS IN ECONOMIC OUTPUT AND MILITARY EXPENDITURES FOR FIVE GREAT POWERS

Cross-National Trends

Figures 3.1, 3.2, and 3.3 illustrate the trends in real national output, real military expenditures, and the shares of military expenditures in national output for the five countries in our data sample. (Russia is omitted in Figures 3.1 and 3.3 and in our discussions of those figures because historical data on Russian national output is unavailable.) To make cross-national comparisons, we use real output and military expenditures series that have been converted to 1982 dollars, as described above.

In 1873, the U.S. economy was more than half again as large as that of its nearest economic rival, Germany, and more than 16 times the size of the smallest economy in the sample, Japan (Figure 3.1). By 1939, strong German and Japanese output growth together with the U.S. Great Depression had shrunk the differentials, but only slightly: The United States was twice as large as Germany and more than 13 times as large as Japan. The French economy, which was approxi-

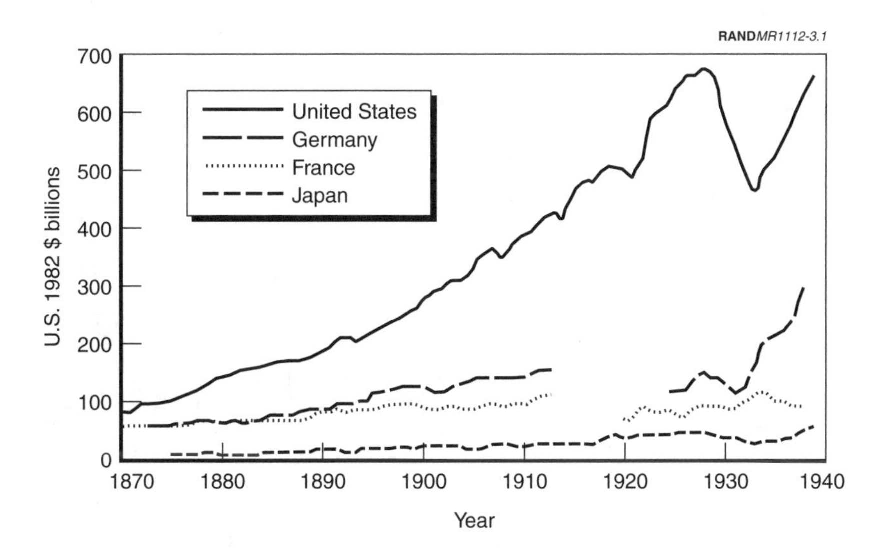

Figure 3.1—Real Output 1870–1939, Four Powers

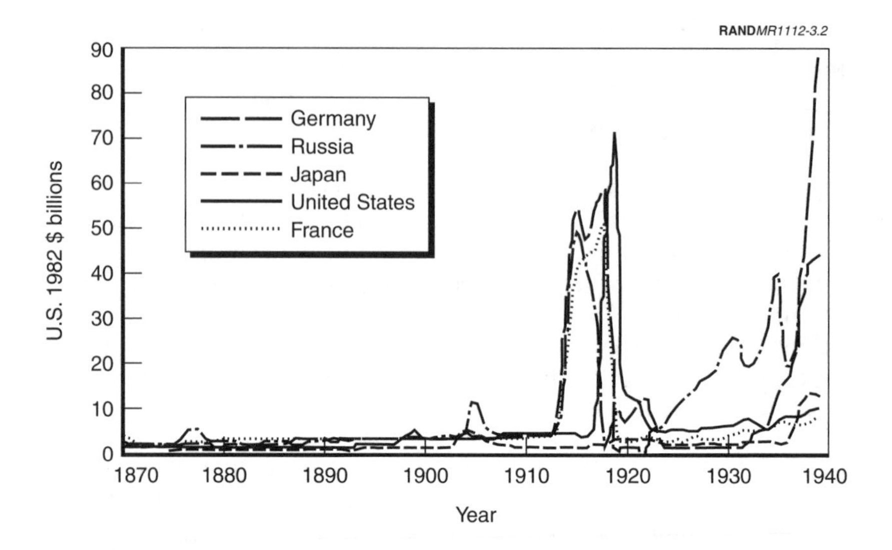

Figure 3.2—Real Military Expenditures 1870–1939, Five Powers

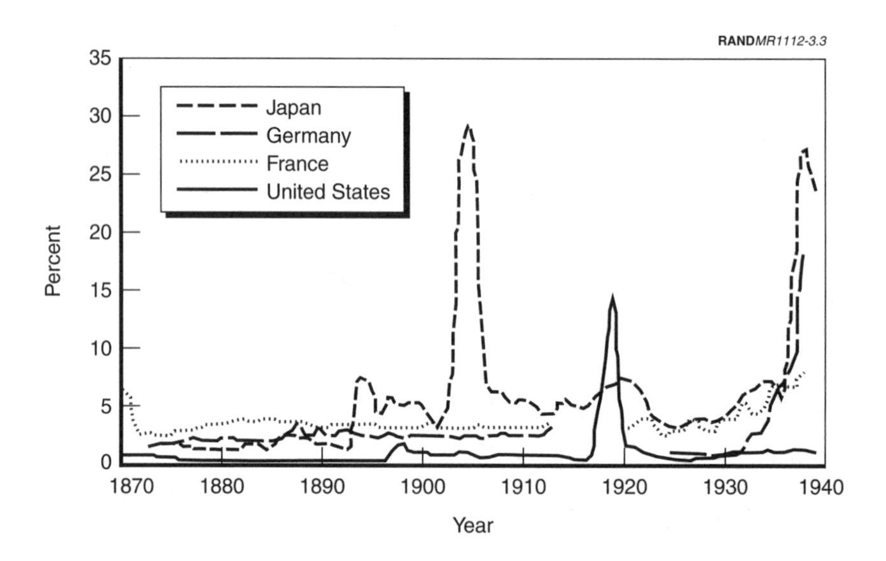

Figure 3.3—Military Expenditures as a Share of Output 1870–1939, Four Powers

mately the same size as Germany's at the beginning of the period, was just one-third as large by 1939.

As Figure 3.2 illustrates, French, Russian, and U.S. real military expenditures peaked during World War I, while German and Japanese military expenditures reached their height during the buildup to World War II. By 1939, Germany was spending more than twice as much on defense as the next biggest spender, Russia, while Japan had overtaken both France and the United States for third place.

As shown in Figure 3.3, on average, the French and Japanese devoted considerably more of their national output to a strong national defense than either Germany or the United States.[4] For example, during the Russo-Japanese War of 1904–1905, almost 25 percent of Japanese output was invested in the military. In 1938, Japanese military expenditures as a share of output topped 25 percent. In the United States, by way of contrast, less than 15 percent of output was devoted to defense even at the height of U.S. involvement in World War I. And by 1929, U.S. military expenditures had fallen back to just 1.5 percent of output.

Individual Country Trends

France. Figure 3.4 allows us to compare trends in real economic output and real military expenditures during the 1870–1939 period. Both series are denominated in 1982 dollars, with output measured on the left-hand scale and military expenditures on the right-hand scale. As shown in the figure, French military spending was growing during the period between the Franco-Prussian War and World War I, but from a relatively low base: Expenditures rose from $1.3 billion in 1872 to $3.7 billion in 1913. Output, on the other hand, rose strongly over the same period: from $54.2 to $104.8 billion. No particular trend in either series is discernible in the chaotic economic conditions of the 1920s, but French military spending began to climb significantly faster than the economy with the rise of Hitler in 1932.

---

[4]For France and Germany, these estimates exclude World War I and the years immediately following.

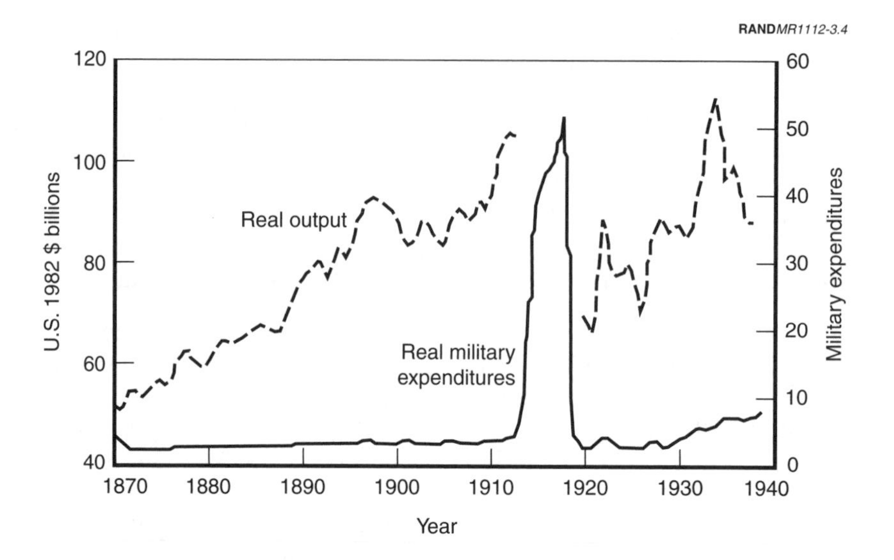

Figure 3.4—French Real Output Versus Real Military Expenditures

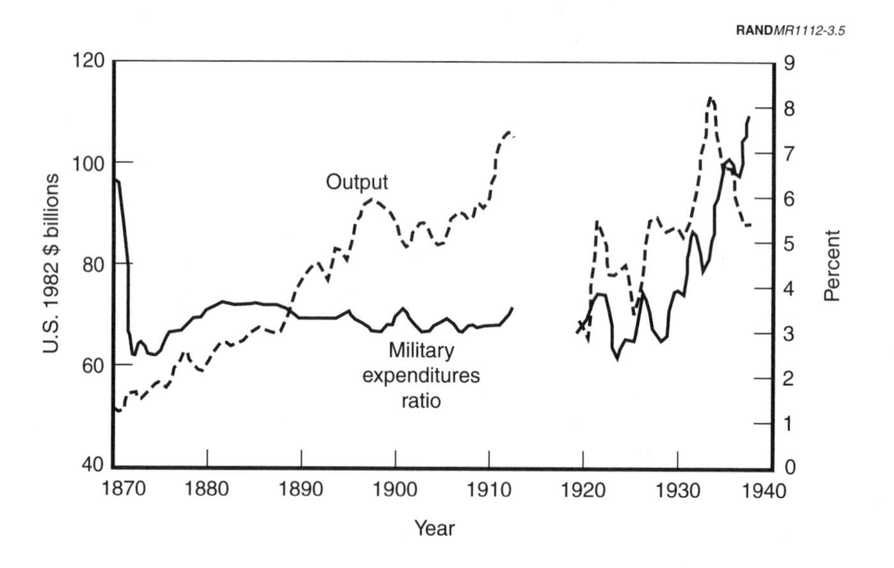

Figure 3.5—French Real Output Versus Military Expenditures-to-Output Ratio

This postwar pattern is seen more clearly in Figure 3.5, where output is again measured on the left axis, but with military expenditures as a percent of output now on the right axis. As a share of output, military spending rose from 3 percent in 1920–1921 to almost 8 percent in 1938. Excepting World War I itself, the share of national output devoted to the military averaged 3.3 percent.

As shown in Figure 3.6, between 1870 and 1913 the share of French CGE devoted to the military also remained fairly constant, averaging approximately 27 percent. Military expenditure shares plummeted at the end of World War I, however, not reaching their prewar percentages again until 1938.

As shown in Figure 3.7, in nonwar years French force levels remained relatively constant, averaging 500,000 men. This was despite large increases in German military personnel before each of the two world wars. Data from Herrmann (1996), designated by white circles, track the Singer and Small (1993) data very closely. One year in which the estimates do differ slightly is 1913, where Herrmann puts French army strength at more than 700,000 men as a result of a 1913 law that

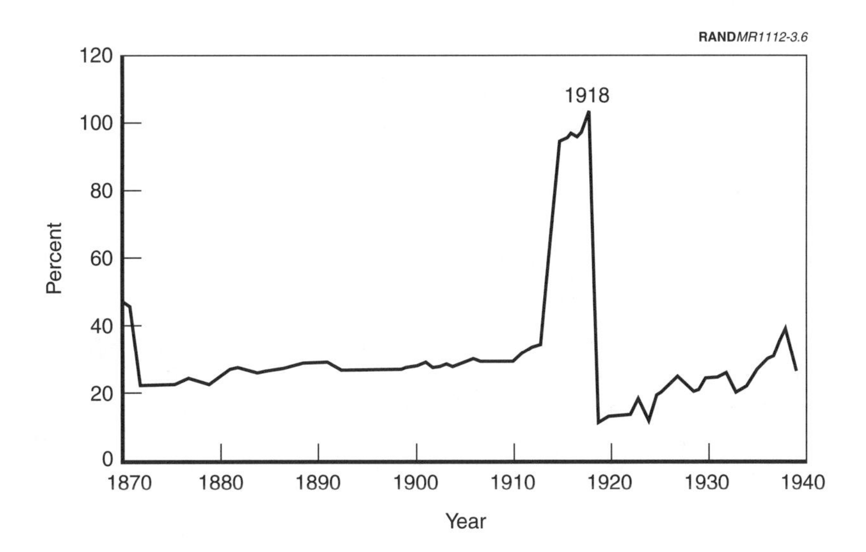

Figure 3.6—French Military Expenditures as a Share of Central Government Expenditure

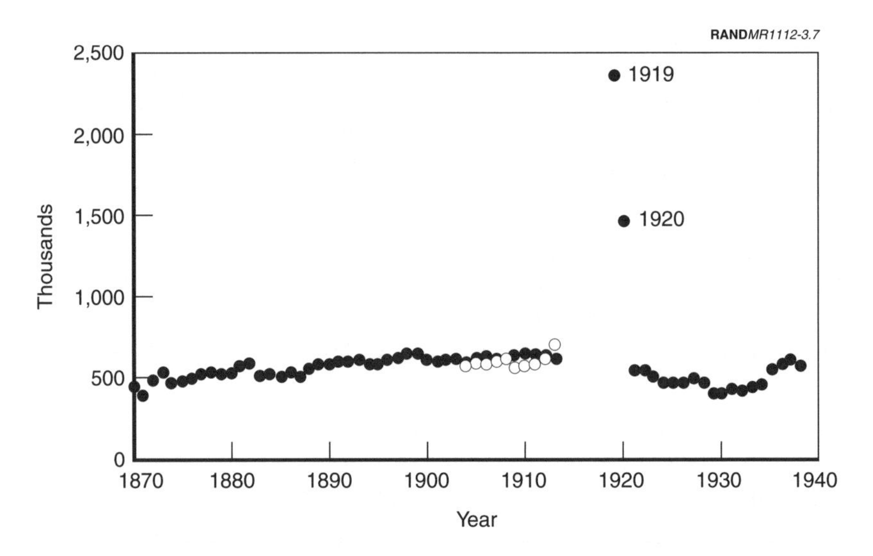

Figure 3.7—French Active-Duty Military Personnel

returned France to a three-year military service standard.[5] This law was passed just two weeks after a German law had raised German troop strength dramatically.

Germany. As indicated by Figure 3.8, German real output rose strongly and steadily between unification in 1872 and the beginning of World War I, rising from $55.8 to $150.2 billion in 1982 U.S. prices. (As before, output is measured on the left-hand axis while military spending is measured on the right.) In fact, World War I and the years of the Weimar Republic can be seen as a brief interruption in an overall strongly upward economic trend.

German real military expenditures prior to World War I grew faster than output but, as in France, did so from a relatively low base: German military spending rose from just $0.8 billion in 1872 to $4.8 billion in 1913. From 1919 to approximately 1931, when German military policy was governed by the Treaty of Versailles, German military spending was effectively isolated from movements in the economy. But this pattern changed dramatically after 1933, when

---

[5]The figure reported by Singer and Small for 1913 is 632,000 men.

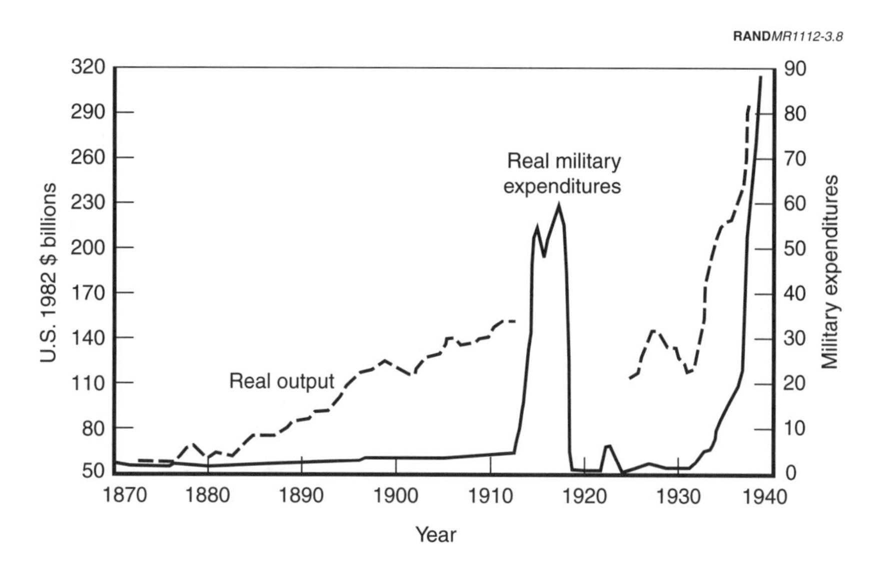

Figure 3.8—German Real Output Versus Real Military Expenditures

both output and military expenditures surged under Adolf Hitler's National Socialist Party.

Figure 3.9 presents a comparison of German real output (left axis) and military expenditures as a share of output (right axis). During most of the sample period, Germany devoted fewer resources to defense as a percentage of output than did France: Except for the massive buildup just prior to World War II, the German military's share of output hovered between 2 and 3 percent as opposed to the French military's 3 to 4 percent. But because Germany's economy grew faster than France's, by the turn of the century the Germans had begun to spend more on defense in absolute terms than France. German military expenditures temporarily fell below those of France as a result of the Weimar Republic's adherence to the Versailles Treaty, but with Hitler's abandonment of the treaty Germany soon regained the lead.

As shown in Figure 3.10, the share of German central government expenditures devoted to defense ranged between 35 and 80 percent in the 1875–1913 period, reaching a high of 77 percent in 1888, the year that Wilhelm II ascended the throne. The average German military expenditures-to-CGE ratio over the period is considerably higher

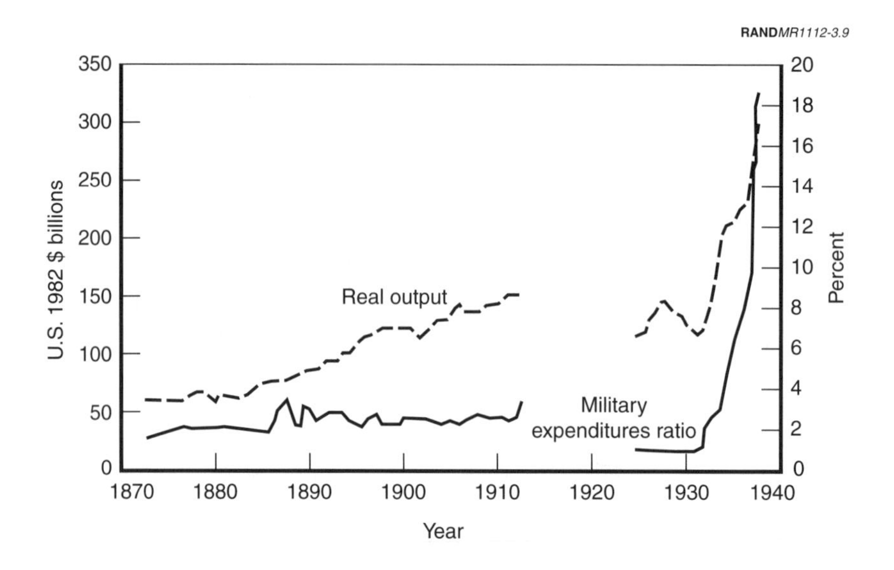

Figure 3.9—German Real Output Versus Military Expenditures-to-Output Ratio

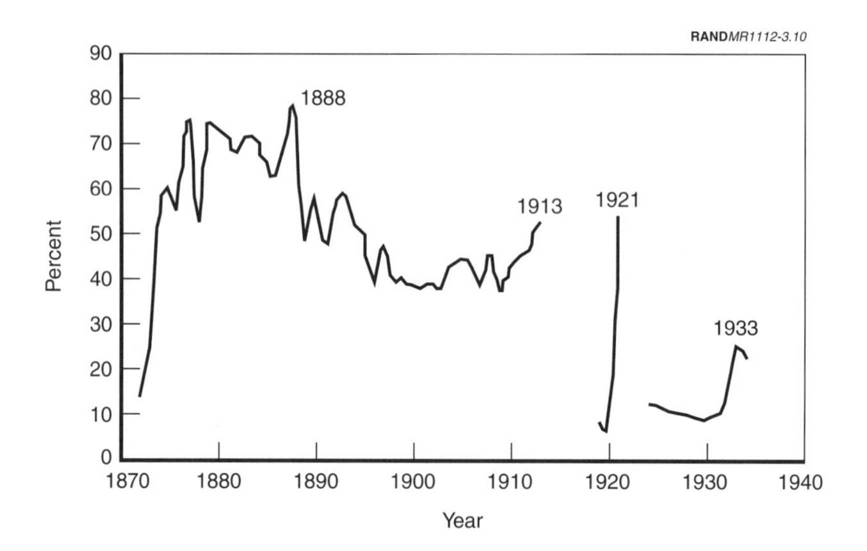

Figure 3.10—German Military Expenditures as a Share of Central Government Expenditure

than that for France, but this is probably misleading. Unlike France, nonmilitary expenditures by German state-level government are large, so that data for the central government tend to overestimate overall government emphasis on defense.

Germany's military personnel strength shows much the same pattern as military expenditures, as shown in Figure 3.11. At unification, the peacetime army was set by the German constitution to 1 percent of the population, and it often did not reach that limit (Herrmann, 1996). In 1912, a changing balance of power on the European continent convinced Germany's leaders that an increase was necessary. Under the army law of 1913, the number of active-duty German army personnel further increased by about a fifth, from approximately 650,000 to 780,000 officers and men. (This pattern is shown clearly in the Herrmann data, again designated by white circles, which exhibit a clear jump in 1912 and again in 1913.)

After Germany's defeat at the end of the World War I, the Versailles Treaty constrained the size of the German military to 100,000. With the rise of Hitler in 1933, however, it experienced a rapid ramp-up, reaching prewar levels by 1938.

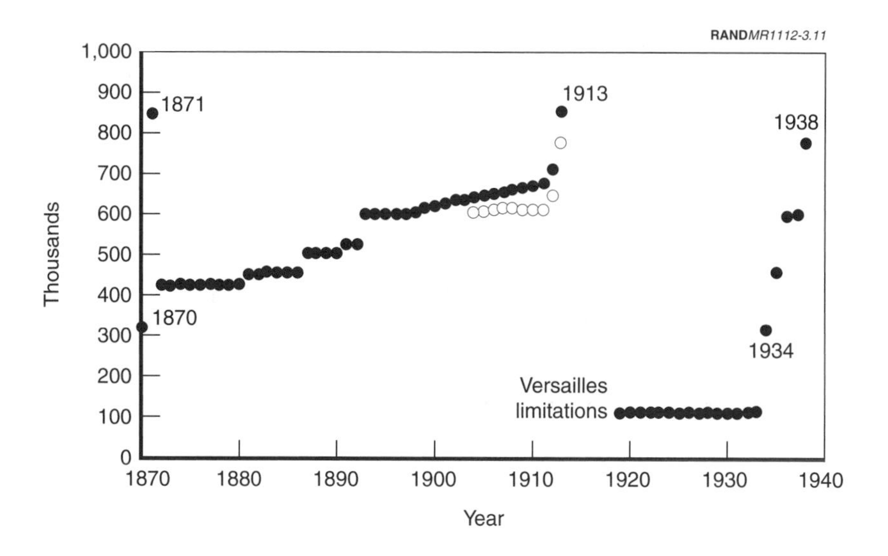

Figure 3.11—German Active-Duty Military Personnel

Japan. As shown in Figure 3.12 (left axis), Japanese real output rose steadily through the end of World War I, climbing from less than $6 billion in 1875 to almost $42 billion in 1919, as measured in 1982 dollars. After a sharp contraction in the early 1930s when Japan shared in the worldwide recession, real output boomed again in the years before World War II, almost doubling in the six years between 1933 and 1939. Excluding war years, Japanese military spending (right axis) also grew steadily until 1936, but it rose even more dramatically than output with the invasion of the Chinese mainland in 1937.

Figure 3.13 presents a similar pattern. Japanese output devoted to defense, measured on the right axis, rose from an average of 2 percent between 1875 and 1893 to an average of 5 percent from 1894 to 1936 (excluding the period of the Russo-Japanese War). During the boom years of the 1920s the military expenditures-to-output ratio fell slightly, but it began rising again in 1930 and jumped dramatically in 1937 with the invasion of China.

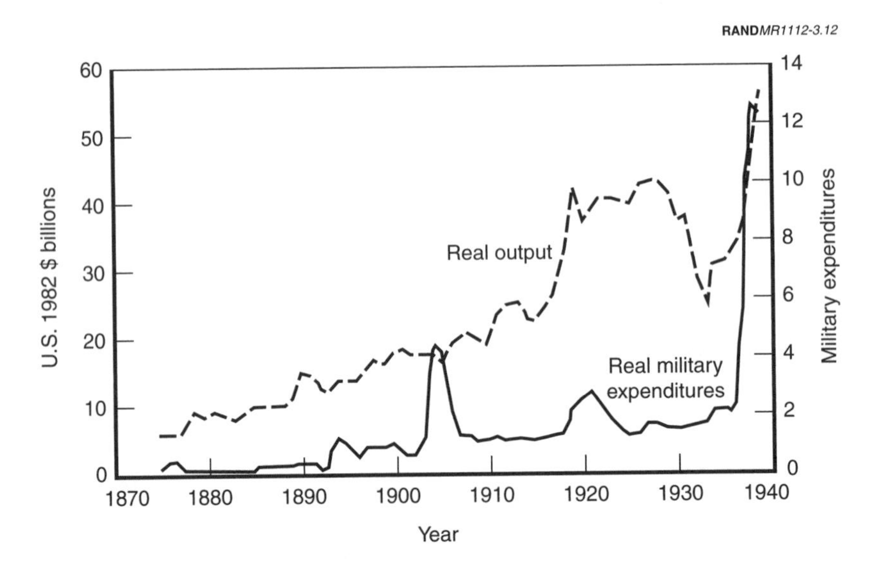

Figure 3.12—Japanese Real Output Versus Real Military Expenditures, 1870–1938

To an even greater extent than the other countries in our sample, the share of Japanese government spending devoted to the military is dominated by periods of war. As shown in Figure 3.14, military expenditures absorbed more than 100 percent of the official government budget during wartime. This was possible because of the creation of extrabudgetary accounts for financing the war that allowed the government to spend more than was allocated in the central government budget.

As shown in Figure 3.15, there were mass mobilizations of Japanese military personnel during the Russo-Japanese war of 1904–1905 and again prior to World War II in 1937–1939. Japan played only a very small role in World War I. In nonwar years, the trend in Japanese military personnel rose slowly but consistently, from 240,000 in 1906 to 330,000 by 1935.

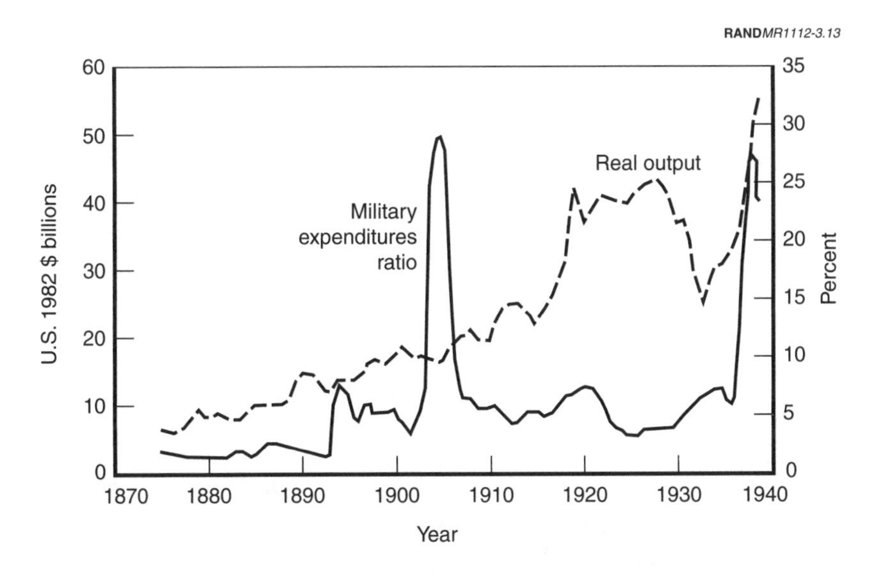

Figure 3.13—Japanese Real Output Versus Military Expenditures-to-Output Ratio

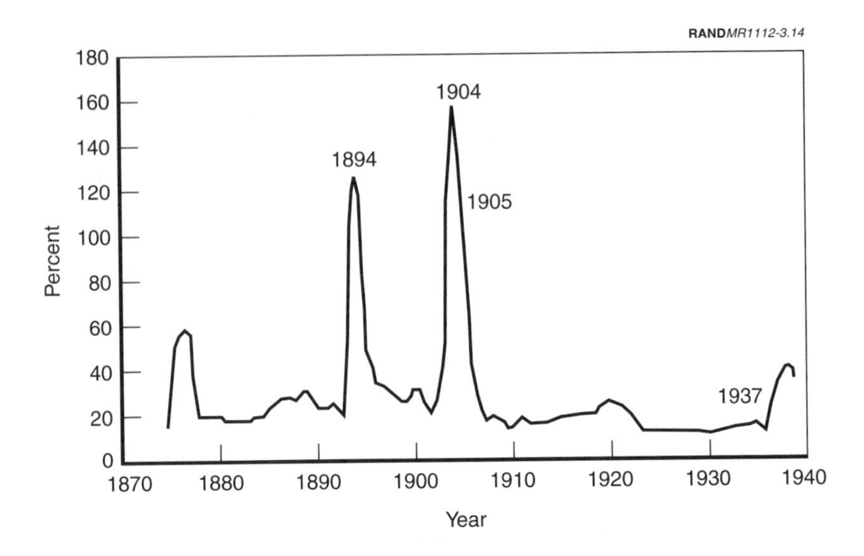

Figure 3.14—Japanese Military Expenditures as a Share of Government Expenditure

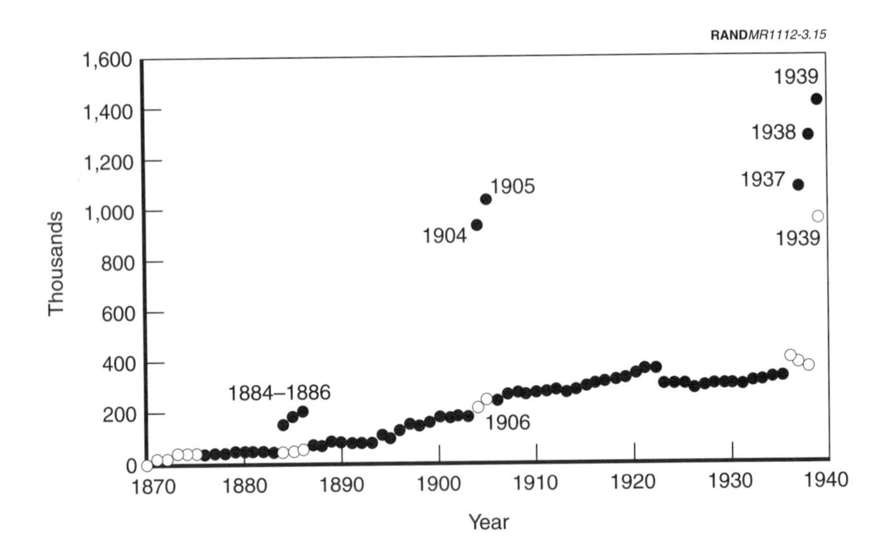

Figure 3.15—Japanese Military Personnel

Russia. As discussed above, no data on Russian GNP or a similar broad measure of national economic output are available for the time period of interest. Accordingly, Figure 3.16 portrays the relationship between Russian iron and steel production (left axis) and real military expenditures (right axis).[6] The trend is strongly positive, but exhibits a significant interruption in the years surrounding World War I and the Russian Revolution of 1917.

The relationship appears to be positive, driven by large increases in both series beginning in the mid-1920s. For the full 1870–1939 sample period, the correlation between the two series is 0.72.[7] It is even higher following World War I, at 0.86 for the period 1920–1939.

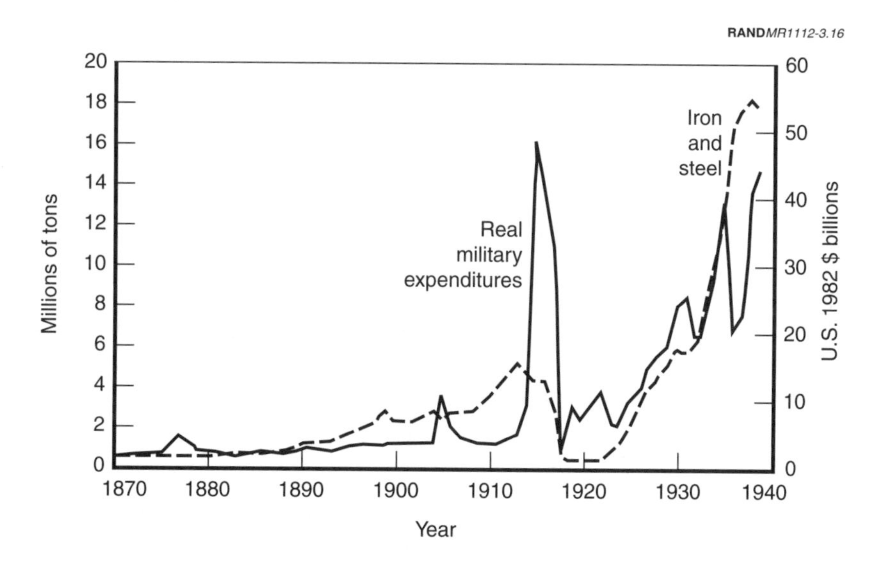

Figure 3.16—Russian Iron and Steel Production and Real Military Expenditures, 1870–1939

---

[6]The high correlation between GDP and iron and steel production for most countries makes this a reasonable proxy; see Table 3.1 above.

[7]For our other proxy for national output, energy consumption, the 1870–1939 correlation with military expenditures is somewhat higher at 0.75.

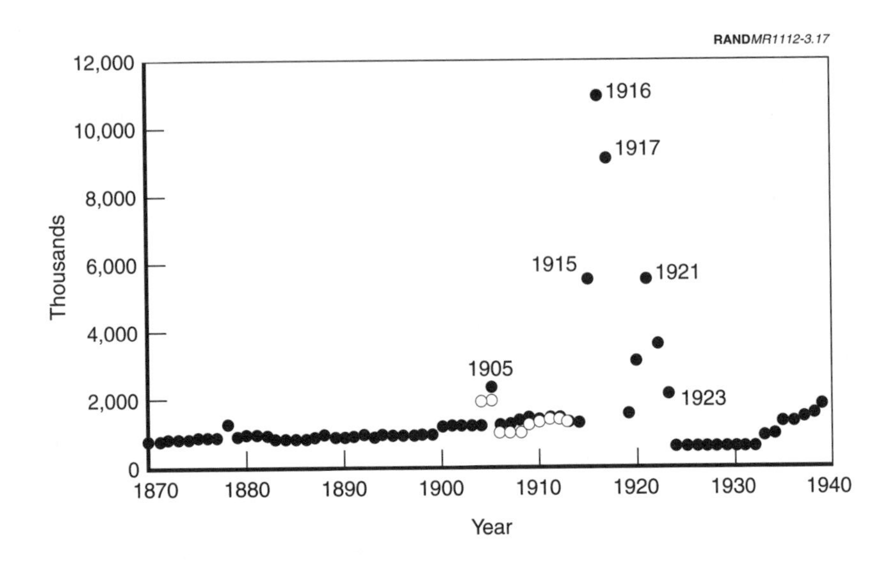

Figure 3.17—Russian Military Personnel

Figure 3.17 shows a steadily rising trend in peacetime Russian military personnel from approximately 700,000 in 1870 to over 1.3 million in 1914. Singer and Small (1993) differ from Herrmann (1996) in their estimate of the size of the 1904 mobilization, but their estimates for the years 1906–1913 match closely. In any case, the prewar trend is dwarfed by the massive mobilizations of 1916 and 1917. Unfortunately for purposes of comparison, we were not able to obtain longer time series estimates from other sources for these years.

United States. The U.S. economy grew strongly over the full sample period, with the prominent exception of the Great Depression in the early 1930s (left axis, Figure 3.18).[8] Measured in 1982 dollars, the U.S. economy grew from roughly $75 billion in 1870 to almost $425 billion in 1913, implying a simple annual growth rate of over 8 percent for more than 40 years. But in contrast to most of the other countries in the sample, increases in U.S. military expenditures were dwarfed by U.S. output growth. As measured on the right axis, during the period

[8]Brief recessions in 1909 and again in the early 1920s show as mere blips on the strong upward trend.

when the other major powers were ramping up their military spending in preparation for World War II, U.S. military expenditures remained resolutely below $10 billion.[9]

The pattern for military expenditures as a share of output closely tracks the pattern in levels, averaging less than one percent in all nonwartime years (Figure 3.19, right axis). Again this contrasts sharply with the other nations in our sample, where nonwartime military expenditures averaged between 2.5 and 4 percent of output.

Figure 3.20 illustrates the U.S. military expenditures-to-CGE ratio. Although the share of U.S. government resources devoted to defense ratcheted up following the Spanish American war, the end of World War I saw a dramatic dropoff in U.S. government support for the military. In 1934, just twenty years after the onset of World War I, the military expenditures-to-CGE ratio was lower than it had been in 1870.

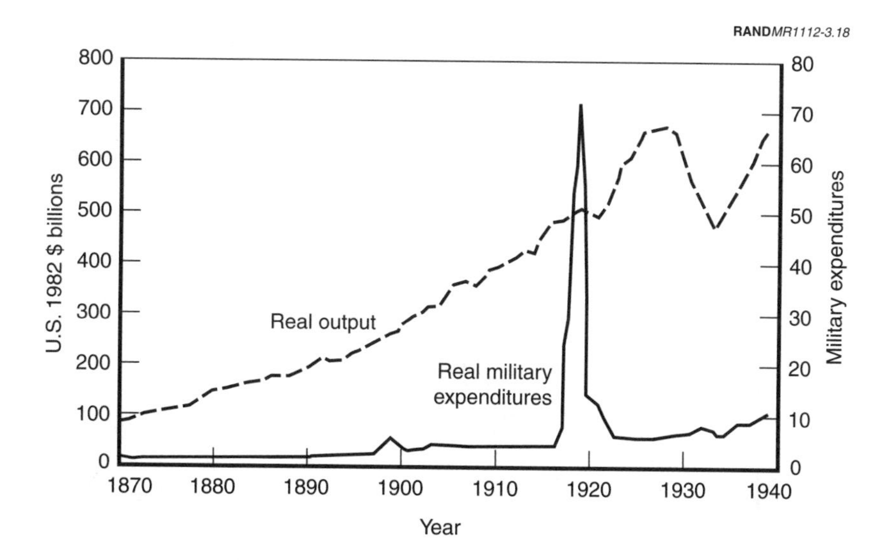

Figure 3.18—U.S. Real Output Versus Real Military Expenditures, 1870–1939

[9]U.S. military expenditure figures do not include U.S. government purchases of equipment for the British Lend-Lease program.

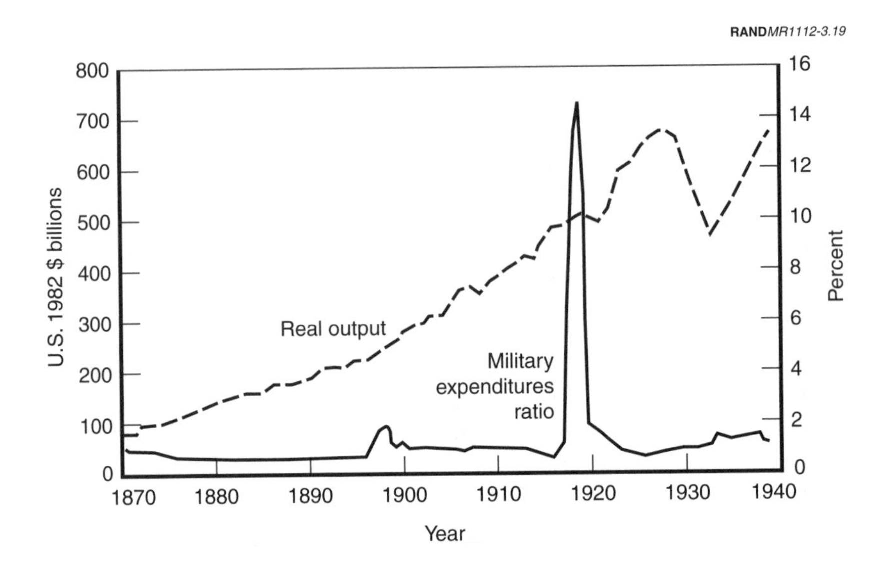

Figure 3.19—U.S. Real Output Versus Military Expenditures-to-Output Ratio

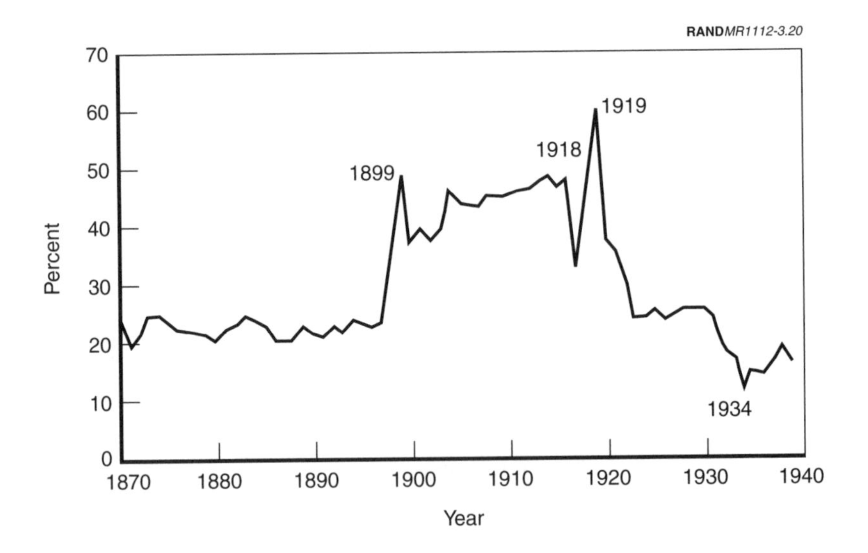

Figure 3.20—U.S. Military Expenditures as a Share of Government Expenditures

Similarly, as shown in Figure 3.21, increases in U.S. active-duty military personnel remained well behind increases in the overall population. Except for the years immediately surrounding World War I (1917–1919), the U.S. armed services rarely rose above 300,000. Significant expansions in military personnel during World War I, for example, were offset by a large postwar demobilization that brought the number of U.S. military personnel back to almost prewar levels by 1922. These numbers did not rise significantly again until the bombing of Pearl Harbor pushed the United States into World War II.

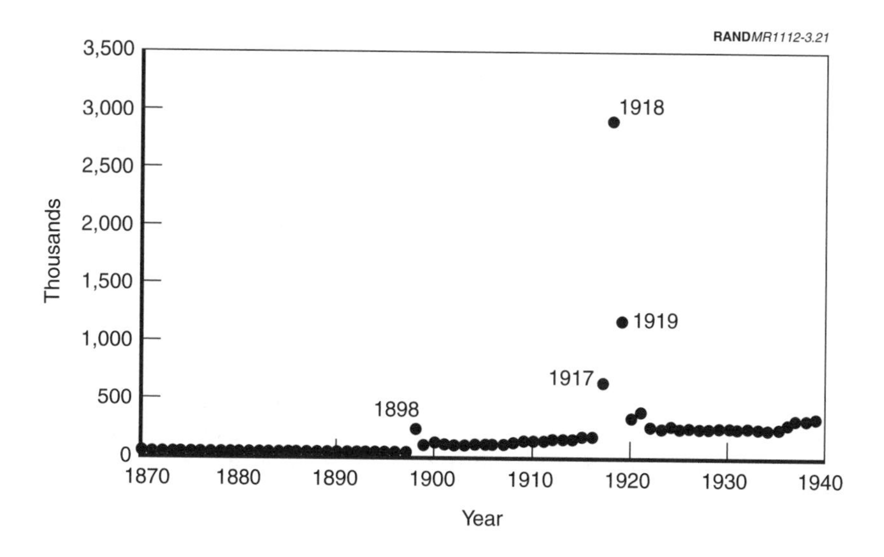

Figure 3.21—U.S. Active-Duty Military Personnel

STATISTICAL ANALYSIS OF MILITARY SPENDING AND ECONOMIC OUTPUT

The graphical analysis above indicates that as their economies grew during the nonwar years before World War I, the five great powers in our sample did generally attempt to match—and only occasionally to outmatch—that growth by increasing their military expenditures. Before World War I, French, German, and U.S. military expenditures generally remained within 1 percent bands centering respectively on

1 percent of output (United States), 3 percent of output (Germany), and 3.5 percent of output (France). Japanese military expenditures as a percentage of output fluctuated considerably more. During the interwar period, however, the share of German, French, and Japanese output devoted to the military trended sharply upward, while in the United States military spending appeared to stagnate at under 2 percent.

What graphical analysis cannot tell us is whether such patterns should be cause for concern. For example, one rather benign interpretation of a positive relationship between economic growth and military expenditures is that as nations become wealthier, they believe they have more to protect. According to this interpretation, growth-led increases in military expenditures are defensive. A less benign interpretation is that greater wealth allows nations to pursue aggressive foreign policy objectives considered unobtainable before. If these foreign policy objectives include, for example, territorial expansion at the expense of neighbors, rapid economic growth should be viewed with more concern by the international community of nations.

In the analysis that follows, we attempt to control for some of the factors other than expansions and contractions in the economy that may have influenced the allocation of national resources toward the military in our five sample countries. In addition to changes in real output, we allow for the possibility that changes in the growth rate of output might also influence military spending decisions. The two variables we condition on are measures of perceived threats from abroad and the openness of the domestic political system. Two alternative models are presented.[10]

Model 1

In our first model, we examine how the respective dependent variables for each nation are affected by changes in four explanatory variables: the level of real national output, the growth rate of real national output, a "threat" variable measured as the active-duty mili-

[10]Regressions on natural log transformations of the military expenditure, output, and threat variables produced results similar to those presented here.

tary personnel of the given nation's major political rivals, and an index of political participation that rates the access of nonelites to political institutions. Defense policymakers are assumed able to respond only with a lag to changes in real output, accelerations in real output growth, and foreign military threats. Lagged values of the dependent variable are also included in each equation in the belief that adjustments to military expenditures are conditioned by the level (or share) of existing allocations.[11] The null hypothesis is that changes in real economic output and real economic growth do not affect military spending decisions.

The equation we estimate for each nation in Model 1 is

$$m_t = c + m_{t-1} * B_M + \sum_j \left(Output_{t-j} * B_{Oj} + Growth_{t-j} * B_{Gj} + Threat_{t-j} * B_{Tj} \right)$$
$$+ Democ_t * B_D + u_t ,$$

where m_t represents real military expenditures or expenditure shares respectively for France, Germany, Japan, Russia, and the United States.[12] The variables c (constant terms), Output (national real output measures), Growth (national real output growth measures), Threat (threat variables), and Democ (democracy indexes) all take the same form. The subscripts t and j are time indexes; for the purposes of our estimation, j is set to 1.

We assume that the disturbance term, u, is correlated across time periods.[13] The assumption of time dependence is based on the belief

[11]We also estimated ordinary least squares regressions for each country with up to 5 lags of output and 5 lags of output growth and no lagged dependent variable. Tests indicated the presence of higher serial correlation—often an indicator of an omitted variable—for every country except Germany. In no case could we reject the hypothesis that the net influence of lagged output and output growth on military expenditures was zero.

[12]The system with military expenditures as a share of output does not include Russia, since Russian national output data are unavailable.

[13]That is, both $Cov(u_{it}, u_{it-1})$ and $Cov(u_{it}, u_{kt})$ are nonzero for countries i and k. This implies that the structure of the time dependence is first-order autoregressive (AR(1)) and that disturbances are contemporaneously correlated across countries. The disturbances are assumed to be stationary, although (unsurprisingly) we cannot formally reject the presence of a unit root in output using augmented Dickey-Fuller tests. Cointegration tests do not suggest that military expenditures and economic output are cointegrated.

that events leading to unplanned military expenditures in one year continue to influence spending decisions the following year.

Because of the correlation between the disturbance term and the lagged dependent variable, m_{t-1}, an ordinary least squares estimation of the system outlined above would result in inconsistent as well as inefficient estimates of the coefficient parameters. We therefore employ an iterative two-step least squares procedure using further lags of the explanatory variables as instruments for m_{t-1}.[14] The sign and significance of the parameter estimates for each country are reported in Tables 3.7 through 3.11. As the democracy variable proved not significant for any country (unsurprising, given its low variance), the regressions reported below exclude it.

France. Table 3.7 presents the findings for France. The signs of the estimated parameters vary across model specifications, and just one coefficient estimate is significant across both specifications. For each specification, the lagged military expenditure variable is statistically significant and positively related to the military expenditure variable in the current period. On average, therefore, increases in French military expenditures in the previous year are good predictors of increases in military expenditures in the next period. There is little support for a positive relationship between output and military expenditures. The sign of the coefficient estimate for lagged French real output is not robust across model specifications, and neither it nor output growth is significantly different from zero in either specification. The threat variable appears to be positive and significant when the dependent variable is real military expenditures, but it changes sign and becomes insignificant when the dependent variable is the military expenditures-to-output ratio. As indicated by the Box-Ljung "Q" statistic, there is evidence of some higher-order serial correlation in the errors for the military expenditures ratio, but not the real military expenditures, specification. Common explanations for the presence of higher-order serial correlation are either the presence of an omitted variable or a high degree of measurement error in the explanatory variables. Either explanation is plausible here.

---

[14]The technique we use was first suggested by Hildreth and Lu (1960); it does not require the absence of missing values in the data.

Table 3.7

France: Sign and Significance of Model 1 Parameter Estimates

	Dependent Variable Is:			
	Real Military Expenditures		Military Expenditures Ratio	
Variable	Sign	Signif	Sign	Signif
Constant	–	No	–	No
Lag Depend	+	Yes	+	Yes
Lag Output	+	No	–	No
Lag Growth	–	No	–	No
Lag Threat	+	Yes*	–	No
Reject Q = 0?	No		Yes	
Adjusted R^2	0.43		0.59	

NOTE: "Yes" denotes significance at the 5 percent level unless marked with an asterisk, which denotes the 10 percent level.

Germany. The model does not do much better at explaining patterns in Germany, as shown in Table 3.8. As with France, the estimated relationship between current and past German military expenditures—whether measured in real terms or as a ratio to national output—is both positive and significant. But coefficients on the level as well as the growth rate of German real output are insignificantly negative in both model specifications. The threat coefficients are also negative, contrary to what most theories would predict, and significantly so when the dependent variable is the military expenditures ratio. Like France, there is evidence of higher-order serial correlation in the errors for the military expenditures ratio specification.

Japan. As reported in Table 3.9, the model does a relatively poor job of explaining Japanese military expenditures. Past military expenditures are both significant and positively related to current expenditures whether measured in real terms or as a ratio to national output, but no other coefficient estimates are statistically significant. There is no evidence of higher-order serial correlation in the errors.

Table 3.8

Germany: Sign and Significance of Model 1 Parameter Estimates

	Dependent Variable Is:			
	Real Military Expenditures		Military Expenditures Ratio	
Variable	Sign	Signif	Sign	Signif
Constant	+	No	+	No
Lag Depend	+	Yes	+	Yes
Lag Output	–	No	–	No
Lag Growth	–	No	–	No
Lag Threat	–	No	–	Yes*
Reject Q = 0?	No		Yes	
Adjusted R^2	0.93		0.42	

NOTE: "Yes" denotes significance at the 5 percent level unless marked with an asterisk, which denotes the 10 percent level.

Table 3.9

Japan: Sign and Significance of Model 1 Parameter Estimates

	Dependent Variable Is:			
	Real Military Expenditures		Military Expenditures Ratio	
Variable	Sign	Signif	Sign	Signif
Constant	+	No	–	No
Lag Depend	+	Yes	+	Yes
Lag Output	+	No	–	No
Lag Growth	–	No	–	No
Lag Threat	–	No	–	No
Reject Q = 0?	No		No	
Adjusted R^2	0.76		–0.11	

NOTE: "Yes" denotes significance at the 5 percent level unless marked with an asterisk, which denotes the 10 percent level.

Russia. As indicated in the section "Data Description," iron and steel production (measured in tons) is used as a proxy for Russian national output. Because iron and steel production is measured in real output units, rather than inflation-adjusted rubles, data on the military expenditures ratio are not available for Russia.

Table 3.10 reports the results for Russia. In contrast to France, Germany, and Japan, movements in past military expenditures do not seem to explain current movements. Lagged values of the output proxy are significant and positive, while output growth is statistically insignificant. Again surprisingly, the threat variable is negative and significant. The "Q" statistic is quite high, suggesting that higher-order serial correlation of the errors is a problem.

Table 3.10

Russia: Sign and Significance of Model 1 Parameter Estimates

	Dependent Variable Is:			
	Real Military Expenditures		Military Expenditures Ratio	
Variable	Sign	Signif	Sign	Signif
Constant	+	Yes	NA	
Lag Depend	–	No	NA	
Lag Output	+	Yes	NA	
Lag Growth	+	No	NA	
Lag Threat	–	Yes	NA	
Reject Q=0?	Yes			
Adjusted R^2	0.58		NA	

NOTE: "Yes" denotes significance at the 5 percent level unless marked with an asterisk, which denotes the 10 percent level.

United States. Table 3.11 presents the econometric findings for the United States. The explanatory power of the model is universally poor: none of the coefficients are statistically significant. We cannot reject the hypothesis of no higher-order serial correlation for the real military expenditures regression, but Q is statistically significant for the military expenditures ratio regression.

Table 3.11

United States: Sign and Significance of Model 1 Parameter Estimates

	Dependent Variable Is:			
	Real Military Expenditures		Military Expenditures Ratio	
Variable	Sign	Signif	Sign	Signif
Constant	–	No	+	No
Lag Depend	+	No	+	No
Lag Output	+	No	+	No
Lag Growth	+	No	+	No
Lag Threat	+	No	–	No
Reject Q = 0?	No		Yes	
Adjusted R^2	0.89		–0.11	

NOTE: "Yes" denotes significance at the 5 percent level unless marked with an asterisk, which denotes the 10 percent level.

Model 2

The relatively weak explanatory power of our first model suggests that it may have been poorly specified. Our second model explicitly allows for a more simultaneous decisionmaking process. Whereas in the first model we assumed that defense policymakers responded (one year later) to external threats in the form of buildups of military personnel, here it is posited that defense policymakers contemporaneously observe each other's military spending decisions and respond accordingly. Such an approach has an additional advantage in that it allows increases in spending by both friends and rivals to influence spending decisions.

The system of simultaneous equations we estimate for Model 2 is

$$M_{it} = C_i + M_{it-1} * B_{Mi} + \sum_j \left(OUTPUT_{it-j} * B_{Oij} + GROWTH_{it-j} * B_{Gij}\right) + \sum_{k \neq i} M_{kt} + U_{it} ,$$

where i and k are country indexes, t and j are time indexes, and all explanatory variables are defined as in Model 1. In this model, however, we assume that the vector of disturbance terms, U, is correlated across countries as well as across time periods.[15] This second assumption derives from the fact that many external events (for example, Austria-Hungary's declaration of war on Serbia) leading to unplanned military expenditures are likely to have affected all four of the countries in our sample contemporaneously. As with the first model, we consider two possible decision variables: real military expenditures and military expenditures as a share of output. Our instrumental variables estimation methodology derives from Fair (1970). Once again, further lags of the explanatory variables are used as instruments for M_{it-1}.

France. The results for France are presented in Table 3.12. Estimated coefficients for three of the explanatory variables are statistically significant: past military expenditures, past output, and past output growth. Consistent with Model 1, the sign on past output is positive, while the sign on past output growth is negative. The effect of contemporaneous German military expenditures on French military spending is not robust across the three specifications and is never statistically significant. The Box-Ljung "Q" test for higher-order serial correlation is not valid for these types of simultaneous systems, so it is not used here.

Germany. As shown in Table 3.13, past military expenditures once again provide most of the explanatory power for current military expenditures. As in Model 1, neither German output measure has a coefficient that differs significantly from zero. Instead, it is the Russian and especially the French contemporaneous military expenditures measures that provide additional explanatory power. Increases in French military spending are associated with increases in German military spending in both specifications of the model.

---

[15]That is, both $\mathrm{Cov}(u_{it}, u_{it-1})$ and $\mathrm{Cov}(u_{it}, u_{kt})$ are nonzero, implying that the structure of the time dependence is first-order autoregressive (AR(1)) and that disturbances are contemporaneously correlated across countries.

Table 3.12

France: Sign and Significance of Model 2 Parameter Estimates

	Dependent Variable Is:			
	Real Military Expenditures		Military Expenditures Ratio	
Variable	Sign	Signif	Sign	Signif
Constant	–	Yes	–	No
Lag Depend	+	Yes	+	Yes
Lag Output	+	Yes	+	Yes*
Lag Growth	–	Yes	–	Yes
German military expenditures	–	No	+	No
Adjusted R^2	0.49		0.81	

NOTE: "Yes" denotes significance at the 5 percent level unless marked with an asterisk, which denotes the 10 percent level.

Table 3.13

Germany: Sign and Significance of Model 2 Parameter Estimates

	Dependent Variable Is:			
	Real Military Expenditures		Military Expenditures Ratio	
Variable	Sign	Signif	Sign	Signif
Constant	–	Yes*	–	Yes
Lag Depend	+	Yes	+	Yes
Lag Output	–	No	+	No
Lag Growth	–	No	–	No
French military expenditures	+	Yes	+	Yes
Russian military expenditures	+	No	NA	
Adjusted R^2	0.96		0.89	

NOTE: "Yes" denotes significance at the 5 percent level unless marked with an asterisk, which denotes the 10 percent level.

Japan. For Japan, Model 2 has much greater explanatory power than Model 1. As shown in Table 3.14, lagged military expenditures are significant across both model specifications, while real output and U.S. military expenditures are significant in the real military expenditures specification. Although statistically significant, the coefficient on real output is negative. The U.S. military expenditures variable, however, is positive as predicted.

Table 3.14

Japan: Sign and Significance of Model 2 Parameter Estimates

	Dependent Variable Is:			
	Real Military Expenditures		Military Expenditures Ratio	
Variable	Sign	Signif	Sign	Signif
Constant	+	No	–	No
Lag Depend	+	Yes	+	Yes
Lag Output	–	Yes	+	No
Lag Growth	–	No	–	No
Russian military expenditures	+	No	NA	
U.S. military expenditures	+	Yes	+	No
Adjusted R^2	0.81		0.50	

NOTE: "Yes" denotes significance at the 5 percent level unless marked with an asterisk, which denotes the 10 percent level.

Russia. The regression results for Russia are presented in Table 3.15. With Russian iron and steel production as the proxy for output, coefficients on output and output growth appear to have no statistically significant relation to real military expenditures. This is not consistent with the Model 1 results. Neither German nor Japanese military expenditures have any significant explanatory power.

Table 3.15

Russia: Sign and Significance of Model 2 Parameter Estimates

	Dependent Variable Is:			
	Real Military Expenditures		Military Expenditures Ratio	
Variable	Sign	Signif	Sign	Signif
Constant	–	No	NA	
Lag Depend	+	Yes	NA	
Output	–	No	NA	
Growth	+	No	NA	
German military expenditures	–	No	NA	
Japanese military expenditures	+	No	NA	
Adjusted R^2	0.84		NA	

NOTE: "Yes" denotes significance at the 5 percent level unless marked with an asterisk, which denotes the 10 percent level.

United States. The U.S. results from Model 2 are presented in Table 3.16. Lagged military expenditures are now the best predictor of current military expenditures, with a strong and significant positive relationship. Real output and real output growth continue to have no significant relation to either real military expenditures or the military expenditures ratio. However, German and Japanese military expenditures are, respectively, positively and negatively related to U.S. military expenditures in the real military expenditures specification.

CONCLUSION

Overall, both our graphical and statistical analysis indicate that the relationship between military expenditures, economic output, and economic output growth varies over time and across countries. Further, our statistical results are not robust to different model specifications. In terms of explanatory power, there is no consistent pattern across models or across countries, although Model 1 is clearly less able to explain movements in Japanese and U.S. military expenditures ratios, while Model 2 does well at explaining move-

Table 3.16

United States: Sign and Significance of Model 2 Parameter Estimates

	Dependent Variable Is:			
	Real Military Expenditures		Military Expenditures Ratio	
Variable	Sign	Signif	Sign	Signif
Constant	–	No	+	No
Lag Depend	+	Yes	+	Yes
Output	+	No	+	No
Growth	+	No	–	No
German military expenditures	+	Yes	+	No
Japanese military expenditures	–	Yes*	+	No
Adjusted R^2	0.90		0.61	

NOTE: "Yes" denotes significance at the 5 percent level unless marked with an asterisk, which denotes the 10 percent level.

ments in both measure of military expenditures for France. For most countries, the strongest predictor of current military expenditures is military expenditures in the immediate past, whether these expenditures are measured in levels or as a share of output. While it is unsurprising that current military spending decisions are heavily influenced by decisions made in the past, this fact sheds little light on why decisions were made in the first place.

Our results indicate that the statistical evidence for a strong relationship between great-power military expenditures and economic output during the 1870–1939 sample period is less than overwhelming. Certainly no conclusive evidence as to the direction of causality between the two has been presented. Threat-based explanations for military spending also receive mixed support from our analysis: While it seems plausible that Germany might respond positively to increases in French military spending, for example, it seems much less plausible that the United States actually *reduced* its military expenditures in response to Japanese spending increases.

In the next chapter, therefore, we provide a more qualitative but no less rigorous analysis of the military expenditures–growth relationship. We begin with a careful analytical construction of three alternative hypotheses about the growth–military expenditures relationship. Then, using a case study methodology, we examine influential national and international events in an effort to determine which of the three hypotheses best explains an individual nation's military spending decisions.

Chapter Four

ALTERNATIVE HYPOTHESES ABOUT THE GROWTH–MILITARY EXPENDITURES RELATIONSHIP

THREE MOTIVES FOR INCREASING MILITARY EXPENDITURES

Chapter Three examined whether states increase their defense expenditures during periods of rapid economic expansion. The empirical evidence provided both there and in the literature is ambiguous on the question of whether states tend to increase their military expenditures during periods of rapid economic growth. Our evidence, moreover, suggests that factors other than the economic wealth of states can account for changes in military spending. Thus, a country's wealth might not explain all of the variation in its defense expenditures.

In this chapter, we take a different tack and try to explain what causes a country's investments to vary. We address this issue in the context of a state's broader foreign policy goals. In particular, we examine the motivations behind a state's decision to raise spending on defense. The chapter presents three hypotheses about a state's motives for increasing military spending. To build our hypotheses, we rely on the international relations literature and its stockpile of theories about the foreign policy behavior of states. While a variety of explanations can determine a state's security policy, we narrow our focus to three hypotheses about a state's military expenditures:

1. States are ambitious and economic growth produces forward-looking foreign policies and thus greater military spending.
2. States are fearful and they increase their military expenditures in response to threats.

3. States use aggressive foreign policies and high levels of military expenditures to deflect domestic troubles.

Hypothesis One (Ambition): A State's Military Spending Varies with Its Economic Power

The ambition hypothesis rests on five assumptions about international politics. First, the international system lacks a central authority to arbitrate disputes among states. In practice, this prevents states from turning to a higher political entity to keep the peace or protect them from aggressive neighbors. Second, states cannot discern the intentions of other states with any amount of certainty. Decisionmakers will always find it difficult to know if other countries harbor benign or malign intentions. Third, all states possess some form of military capabilities giving them the ability to inflict harm on their neighbors. Fourth, the pursuit of additional economic and military power represents the highest goal of states. Here, power refers to a state's material capabilities. Lastly, a state's wealth shapes its foreign policy objectives. According to ths assumption, states have an insatiable appetite for power that is constrained only by their material resources. As such, the greater a state's economic capabilities, the larger its foreign policy ambitions.

Taken together, these assumptions produce three common behaviors among states. In an anarchic international environment, where there is no centralized authority, states follow the principle of self-help. This condition forces states to protect their interests. Furthermore, countries will seek opportunities to maximize their relative economic and military power.[1] Both life under anarchy and the

[1]See, for example, Morgenthau (1978); Mearsheimer (1990, pp. 5–56); Mearsheimer (1994/95, pp. 5–49); Huntington (1993, pp. 68–83); Zakaria (1998, pp. 13–43); and Zakaria (1992, pp. 1771–1798). Interested readers should note that these authors disagree on whether the lack of a centralized authority or human nature drives a state to maximize its relative power. These "drivers" of expansion, which are often posited as alternative explanations in the literature, may in fact vary more as a result of the level of analysis than as a consequence of any ontological differences. Further, it is possible to demonstrate that maximization of relative power can occur as *the* "single-exit" outcome even if the agents are assumed to have no more than the minimal preferences associated with self-preservation. (For an extended demonstration of this proposition, see Tellis (1994).) Such demonstrations, in effect, suggest that even minimally egoistic assumptions about security on the part of self-regarding political entities can give rise to expansionist and predatory behaviors that are simply indistin-

lust for domination found in human nature drive states to pursue more power. Thus, when occasions arise for states to improve their position vis-à-vis their neighbors, states are almost certain to seize them. Finally, while states possess an unquenchable thirst for power, their foreign policies often reflect a conscious strategic calculation about the costs and benefits of undertaking action to enhance their international position. States attempt to change the international system for their benefit by altering existing international agreements, redrawing the boundaries of spheres of influence and territorial expansion when the benefits exceed the costs (Gilpin, 1981). According to Frederick the Great, states design their foreign policies to follow the "permanent principle of rulers," which is "to extend as far as their power permits."[2]

Hypothesis 1: The greater a state's economic wealth, the larger its military expenditures.

The ambition hypothesis contends that military expenditures are both directly and indirectly a positive function of economic growth. As illustrated in Figure 4.1, economic growth tends to increase the extractive abilities of states through taxation or state ownership or control over resources. Greater resource availability heightens foreign policy ambitions, which are translated into increased military expenditures. But economic growth also tends to increase the centralization of government, which in turn increases the power of the state, heightens foreign policy ambitions, and so leads to increased military expenditures.

What Kind of Evidence Would Confirm the Ambition Hypothesis?

The ambition hypothesis suggests three possible routes of empirical testing. One avenue of testing involves a direct examination of the

---

guishable from other actions rooted in an unquenchable thirst for power. To keep the analysis and the testing of data simple, however, this monograph does not investigate any hypotheses that posit power maximization to result simply from the desire for minimal security, since that would involve an unmanageable blurring of the effects deriving from either ambition or fear. Consequently, these motives are treated as alternatives and their consequences hypothesized to be separate and distinguishable as well.

[2]Frederick the Great's comment is quoted in Zakaria (1992, p. 19).

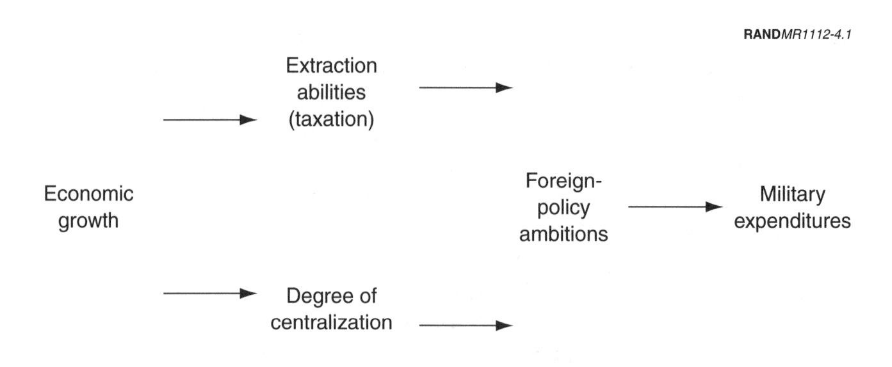

Figure 4.1—The Ambition Hypothesis

relationship between economic wealth and military spending. We would expect states seeing growth in their economic capabilities to translate these resources into greater military spending. Increases in economic indicators, such as industrial capacity (GNP or GDP), energy consumption, iron and steel production as well as population, should correlate positively with a state's military expenditures (Kennedy, 1984). Because, as noted in Chapters Two and Three, military expenditures themselves may spur economic growth, ideally this correlation would be observed with a lag. That is, we would see increases in output *before* increases in military expenditures.

An additional test of this hypothesis entails analyzing an intermediate variable: The ability of states to translate economic power into military power.[3] States differ in their capacity to extract economic gains for government expenditures. Taxation capabilities will affect how much wealth policymakers can allocate for military expenditures. Scholars also argue that more-centralized governments are better able to channel a state's affluence into military investments (Organski and Kugler, 1980).

Examining the behavior of states experiencing economic growth is another way to assess the usefulness of the ambition argument. Typically, states with modernizing economies should attempt to extend their influence over international events. Wealthy states

---

[3]For a detailed examination of the anatomy of this process, see Tellis et al. (2000).

should be more aggressive than poor states, seizing opportunities to increase their power. Concerns over the availability of trading markets, for example, might lead states to acquire colonies or form alliances. When they accumulate wealth, states might also endeavor to change existing spheres of influence and to alter existing international agreements to their advantage.

Hypothesis Two (Fear): A State's Military Expenditures Depend on Its Level of Security[4]

The fear hypothesis shares three assumptions with the previous hypothesis about ambitious states. First, both arguments assume states are the most important political unit in the international system. Uncertainty about the intentions of other states represents a second assumption shared by both hypotheses. The third common assumption is that all states possess enough offensive weaponry to harm other states. Finally, unlike the ambition argument, the fear hypothesis assumes that a state's foreign policy is not driven by the lust for power, but instead is motivated by a search for survival. Military expenditures, therefore, are a function of a state's insecurity. The greater the level of threat to a state's security, the higher the level of military spending.

When combined, these assumptions produce three common behavior patterns among states. Responding to the lack of centralized authority in international politics, states adhere to the self-help standard. Because there is no government over governments, states must take measures to provide for their own security. Moreover, without the protection of some higher authority, and without the ability to know for certain the intentions of their neighbors, states strive to maintain their relative power. States jealously guard the balance of power and cast a suspicious eye on countries that try to surpass other members of the international system in economic and military capabilities. This contrasts with the ambition hypothesis, where absolute, not relative, power determines foreign policy and military spending. Lastly, policymakers decide on an appropriate

---

[4]See Waltz (1979).

security policy by estimating the level of threat posed by other states (Walt, 1987, 1995).

States look at four indicators to determine whether their neighbors are threatening (Walt, 1987):

1. **The aggregate economic and military capabilities of other states.** All things being equal, states with greater economic wealth and larger militaries appear more threatening.
2. **Geography.** When choosing security policies, decisionmakers consider how terrain might aid or hamper conquest by potential enemies. Topographical features like mountain ranges or large bodies of water improve a state's chances against conquest and add to its overall feeling of security. Policymakers also worry more about states nearby than those a continent away.
3. **The offense-defense balance.**[5] The anarchic world of international politics conditions states to evaluate the military landscape carefully. States not only scrutinize the quantitative measure of their competitors' military power but also consider the types of military missions their opponents might undertake against them. More generally, states take an interest in whether military technology aids or hampers the seizure of territory. When conquest is easy, the offense maintains the advantage. While known technologies usually determine whether offensive or defensive military missions are advantageous, states occasionally misjudge the offense-defense balance.
4. **Military posturing and rhetoric.** In addition to objective appraisals of technology and perceptions of the offense-defense balance, policymakers consider states espousing nationalistic or revolutionary political ideologies as possessing offensive advantages.[6]

---

[5]The key works on the offense-defense balance include Jervis (1976); Quester (1977); Van Evera, (1984a); Van Evera (1984b); Van Evera (1997); Glaser and Kaufmann (1998); Glaser (1994/95); and Jones (1995).

[6]The *levy en masse* in Revolutionary France, for example, stemmed in large part from a population motivated by patriotism. Armed with the first mass army of the modern era, France almost succeeded in its early nineteenth-century bid for European hegemony. For a discussion of why states differ in their determination to fight and win wars, see Castillo (forthcoming).

States also determine threats by gauging the intentions of their potential competitors. Unfortunately, ascertaining a state's motives is often a tricky endeavor.[7] Consider British attempts to discern the motivations behind the German decision to engage in a naval buildup before World War I (Kennedy, 1984). Some British policymakers viewed a larger navy as a signal of German aggression, while others interpreted this event as an indication of Berlin's insecurity. Behavior in a crisis can provide one indicator of a state's intentions. By asking the following questions, decisionmakers attempt to gain some insights into the motives of other countries: Which state precipitated the crisis? Did any of the states involved use the crisis as an excuse for territorial aggrandizement?[8] Moreover, a state's ideological disposition can provide clues about its intentions.[9] Those states championing aggressive nationalist doctrines will appear more threatening. Likewise, governments with similar ideological convictions will seem more suitable as allies than as enemies.

Hypothesis 2: The greater the level of international security threats perceived by a state's policymakers, the higher a state's military expenditures.

As illustrated in Figure 4.2, the fear hypothesis implies that states increase their military spending primarily in response to their perception of external threats. According to this hypothesis, very poor states who fear their neighbors would devote a much larger share of their national and budgetary resources to defense than would

---

[7]Here we use the words intentions and motives interchangeably. However, we recognize that the international relations literature treats these terms as analytically distinct. For more on the difference between intentions and motives, see Jervis (1970) and Glaser (1997).

[8]For a discussion of how states might categorize their neighbors, see Jervis (1970).

[9]Aggressive ideologies can sometimes drive security-seeking states to misperceive the intentions of one another and generate spirals of insecurity. On the potential for conflict among states only seeking security, see Jervis (1978). Jervis (1976) also outlines the dynamics behind spirals of hostility. Glaser (1997) has elaborated on these issues most recently. For a different perspective on how the interaction among states can sometimes lead to either amicable or hostile relationships, see Wendt (1999).

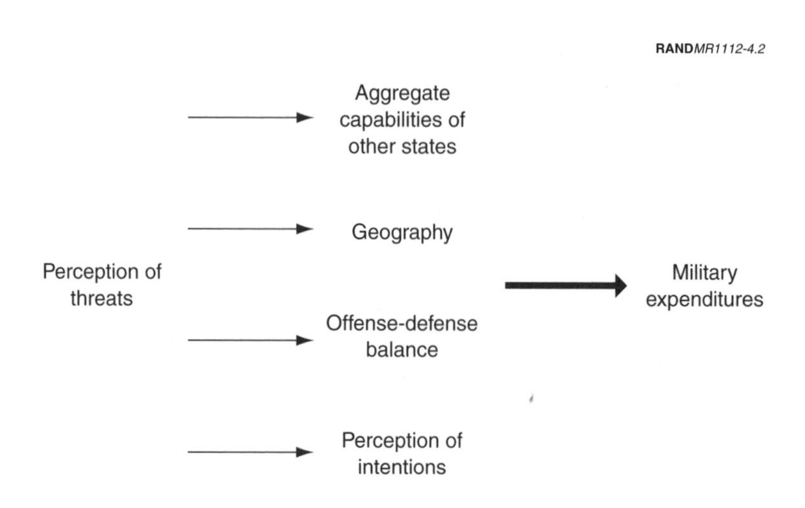

Figure 4.2—The Fear Hypothesis

wealthy countries who have more confidence in their own security. This argument is less likely to hold with respect to levels than to shares, however, as wealthy countries simply have a larger resource pie available to apportion.

What Kind of Evidence Would Confirm the Fear Hypothesis?

If the fear hypothesis is valid, we should see policymakers reacting to threatening states by raising military expenditures. Increases in the four threat indicators should correlate positively with investments in armed forces. Below we outline the expected relationships:

1. **Aggregate capabilities.** The greater the relative increase in the aggregate capabilities of other states, the greater the likelihood decisionmakers will increase military expenditures. These aggregate capabilities include economic wealth (GDP and industrial capability), population, and size of the military.
2. **Geography.** The fewer the geographical barriers against conquest a state possesses, the higher the likelihood it will increase its military expenditures.
3. **The offense-defense balance.** The more military technology or ideology makes conquest easier, the greater the likelihood that states will increase their military expenditures.

4. **Perception of aggressive intentions.** The more aggressive a state's policymakers perceive the intentions of other nearby states to be, the higher the probability they will increase military expenditures. Ideology and peacetime behavior represent two possible indicators of aggressive intentions.

Hypothesis Three (Legitimacy): Government Leaders Use Foreign Policy to Deflect Problems at Home

Our first two hypotheses explain a state's behavior with reference to the international system. These perspectives downplay the domestic determinants of foreign policy. While foreign policy often reacts to dangers from abroad, it can also react to troubles at home. To deflect attention from internal difficulties, governments sometimes create external threats. In this view, international conflict grows out of a state's societal difficulties rather than ambition or fear.

This hypothesis contends that when governments perceive an erosion in their domestic legitimacy, they adopt expansionist foreign policies and increase military expenditures. Regimes see expansion as an instrument to deflect attention from their domestic failures and sustain their government's legitimacy. An expansionist foreign policy includes military buildups, diplomacy based on brinksmanship, and the seizure of territory by force.

While no single theory of the domestic sources of foreign policy exists, several common themes emerge to provide the building blocks for our hypothesis. In particular, we borrow from Simmel's (1955) discussion of diversionary war and Snyder's (1991) insights into the influence of interest groups on a state's foreign policy.[10] As in the first two hypotheses, this argument rests on a few simple assumptions. First, the foremost goal of governments is maintaining their political power. Political leaders realize the continuation of their regime depends on its legitimacy. Governments that lose the faith of the governed face a greater chance of losing power. Keeping the reins of power tops the list of preferences for state leaders. Sec-

---

[10]The classic statement on the diversionary war tactics of governments remains Simmel (1955).

ond, a state's interest groups attempt to alter foreign policy to their advantage. Different societal factions have a stake in influencing where their state directs trade, sends its armed forces, or makes alliance commitments.

The third assumption is that policymakers consider both domestic and international threats to their security when deciding on an appropriate foreign policy. Alliances formed to counter the domestic upheaval of revolution are not uncommon occurrences in international politics. In 1833, for instance, the reactionary regimes of Austria, Prussia, and Russia signed the Treaty of Munchengratz and agreed to defend one another against the growing forces of political liberalization. Although Vienna and St. Petersburg regularly competed for influence in the Balkans, they set aside their differences to keep peace at home.

Under these assumptions we expect governments to react to their domestic and international environments in three ways. First, government leaders respond to an erosion in domestic support by adopting aggressive foreign policies. In situations where regimes face the possibility of removal from power, they weigh the benefits of a more assertive security policy versus its possible costs. Foreign policy elites understand they run the risk of war by engaging in more bellicose international behavior, such as rapid military buildups or diplomacy based on brinksmanship. Unable to mollify different domestic constituencies, governments rely on international events to garner a consensus in support of their leadership. External threats to a state's security can overshadow the failures of the ruling regime. Fears about a country's future in the international system contain a sense of urgency that persuades dissident elements to rally around the current government.

Second, to generate a broad national consensus for their foreign policy aims, governments ally with interest groups. No single entity, including the government, can successfully hijack a state's foreign policy. Partnerships with different societal interests raise the probability governments will successfully implement a diversionary foreign policy. Without support from industrialists or the military, international expansion would never get off the ground. Interest groups ally with regimes to pursue their own particular goals. For example, militaries may gain from expansion because they receive greater resources, allowing them to pursue offensive military strategies, their preferred plan of action. Industrialists might also profit from a military buildup driven by expansion.

Finally, regimes and their special interest allies rely on three forms of propaganda to engender statewide support for expansionist foreign policies: nationalism, security myths, and threatening enemy images. Political leaders cannot guarantee that their more aggressive stance in international relations will translate into a more popular government. As such, regimes go to great lengths to convince their constituents that international events demand larger militaries and aggressive diplomacy (Snyder, 1991). The likelihood of inculcating a population with these ideas depends on the type of government in power. Because they possess institutions independent of the government to evaluate foreign policy and because they do not maintain a monopoly on the flow of information, democracies are less likely to fall victim to security propaganda. Alternatively, nondemocratic states possess fewer self-evaluative organizations and, therefore, are more likely to take the government at its word on security matters.

Nationalism. One of the tools in a government's propaganda toolbox is nationalism, defined as a political ideology arguing that each nation or ethnic group deserves its own state (Gellner, 1983). Nationalism represents a defining feature of modern international politics. Several scholars, such as Gellner (1983), contend nationalism made industrialization possible by convincing individuals that they belonged to a larger political entity and that they should embrace the responsibilities inherent in this collective identity. Nationalism's emphasis on the political sovereignty of ethnic groups first made mass armies and extensive compulsory education efforts possible. Since the French Revolution, defending ethnic homelands has become a common theme of international conflict. To garner popular endorsement for expansionist security policies, regimes frequently define international politics along nationalist lines. Nationalism indoctrinates members of society to bear the potential costs and risks of aggressive foreign policies.

Security myths. In addition to nationalism, governments propagate myths about their state's security to convince their constituents that an expansionist foreign policy is both necessary and effective.

Security myths are age-old instruments of propaganda and usually take two forms: paper tiger and domino images (Snyder, 1991).

Paper tiger images suggest that although adversaries might possess formidable military capabilities, they lack the resolve to use them. Because other states are afraid of risking war, so the argument goes, they will likely react to aggressive policies by making concessions. Driven by the fear of war, the bark of other states is much worse than their supposed bite. This type of reasoning tends to lower the costs of belligerent diplomacy. Since they confront paper tigers, states can achieve their aims more effectively through threats to use force than cooperation.

Domino theories are another popular security myth. According to domino logic, states must increase their military capabilities and defend distant commitments to deter potential aggressors. Retreats on small issues ruin a state's credibility with its allies and demonstrates to its enemies a lack of resolve to use force. Domino images characterize international politics in a highly competitive light. While paper tiger images exaggerate the potential benefits of an aggressive foreign policy, domino images make expansion a necessity.

Threatening images. Threatening images of potential enemies are a final propaganda tool. During war, states typically try to dehumanize their enemies. When directed against those who allegedly exhibit inhumane behavior, individuals find it easier to participate in organized violence. Regimes implementing expansionist foreign policies understand this tendency. A state's population is more likely to endorse an aggressive security policy when government leaders cast adversaries as subhuman or capable of unspeakable atrocities. These threatening images serve two purposes. On one hand, these images lower the moral restraints individuals might hold against using force in international politics. On the other hand, dehumanizing images paint potential opponents as inherently aggressive and innately unreasonable—characteristics that preclude cooperation.

Hypothesis 3: When governments perceive a potential loss to their legitimacy, they will implement an expansionist foreign policy and increase military expenditures.

Under the legitimacy hypothesis, economic growth affects military spending only insofar as it affects the perceived legitimacy of the government. To the extent that economic growth tends to increase legitimacy, by allowing for increased provision of social services, etc., we would expect the legitimacy hypothesis to lead to a negative relationship between economic growth and military expenditures. As shown in Figure 4.3, indicators that an expansionist foreign policy (and attendant increases in military spending) derive from a government's attempt to secure its legitimacy include diversionary tactics, security myths, and the type of governmental regime.

What Kind of Evidence Would Confirm the Legitimacy Hypothesis?

1. **Diversionary tactics.** The rise in domestic strife should correlate with a greater level of international security competition for a state.
2. **Alliances between governments and interest groups.** When a government's legitimacy erodes, it will ally with interest groups to implement an expansionist foreign policy.
3. **Spread of security myths.** When domestic support for a regime diminishes, government leaders will use nationalist propaganda and myths about a state's vulnerability and create demonizing images of potential opponents
4. **Regime type.** The more undemocratic a state's foreign policy decisionmaking, the greater the likelihood government leaders will succeed in cultivating domestic support for expansion.

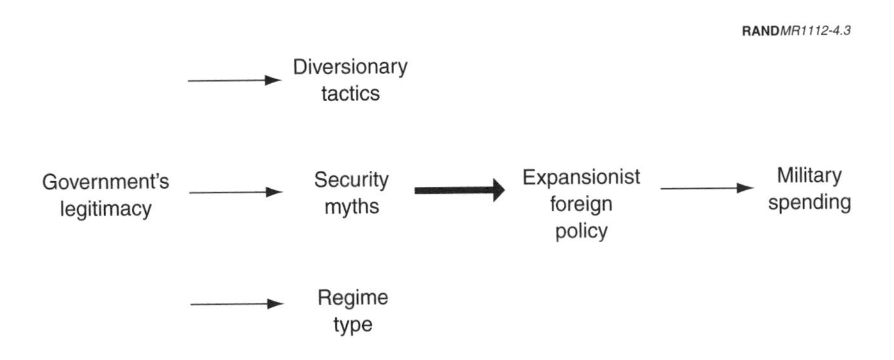

Figure 4.3—The Legitimacy Hypothesis

CONCLUSION

In this chapter we have outlined three causal explanations for the variation in a state's military spending. The ambition hypothesis argues that states experiencing rapid economic growth acquire greater international ambitions and thus increase their rates of military spending. The fear hypothesis argues that states increase their military expenditures when they face increased threats to their security. The legitimacy hypothesis argues that governments that believe their survival is threatened by domestic opposition use an aggressive foreign policy and higher levels of military spending to garner more support at home.

The graphical and statistical evidence presented in Chapter Three allowed us to conduct a partial examination of the ambition and fear hypotheses for each country. A lack of data ruled out an examination of the legitimacy hypothesis. While the statistical evidence for the full period is highly ambiguous, the graphical evidence is consistent with both the ambition and fear hypotheses for certain countries at certain times. In particular, during the economic expansion of the late 1930s, France, Germany, and Japan all significantly increased their military expenditures.[11] In the next chapter, we conduct case studies of particular historical episodes, allowing us to better discriminate between the hypotheses.

---

[11]As we note in Chapter Two, it is not clear whether the expansion drove the expenditures or vice versa.

Chapter Five

HISTORICAL CASE STUDIES OF THE ALTERNATIVE HYPOTHESES

This chapter presents five short case studies of great-power military spending from 1870 to 1939. These historical sketches serve two purposes, one descriptive and the other explanatory. In terms of description, the historical discussion depicts the major trends in the military expenditures of France, Germany, Japan, Russia, and the United States during their periods of economic takeoff.[1] The case studies illustrate the changes in each state's strategic environment in this era.

To explain these trends, we attempt to isolate the driving forces behind each great power's security policy. Each hypothesis presents a different motive for rising military expenditures. Using the three hypotheses from the previous chapter, we try to determine whether military spending varied with growing international ambitions (the ambition hypothesis), security threats from other states (the fear hypothesis), or efforts to divert attention from domestic turmoil (the legitimacy hypothesis). We view the historical case studies offered in this chapter as a preliminary test of the three hypotheses. The goal of the analysis is not to provide the final word on the determinants of great-power military spending but rather to test the plausibility of these three accounts. From the historical case studies we determine whether these hypotheses merit use in a future study.

---

[1]In most cases we use the data sources referenced in Chapter Three, converted to 1982 U.S. dollars where appropriate, for our calculations. However, in cases where currency conversion or U.S. dollar deflation may be misleading, we use sources cited in the text.

We organize the discussion by dividing each case study into three different periods based on significant events: the era after the Franco-Prussian War ending with the departure of German Chancellor Otto von Bismarck (1870–1890); the era before World War I (1891–1913); and the era before World War II (1919–1939). For every era, we outline the pattern in military spending and offer a possible explanation for these expenditures.

Throughout most of the full sample period, the French case appears to validate the fear hypothesis. In this instance, security threats and not economic growth best explain increases in military expenditures. A glance at the empirical record in Germany, Japan, Russia, and the United States offers mixed support for all three hypothesis. In these four cases, rapid economic growth rates correlate positively with higher rates of military spending, evidence in favor of the ambition hypothesis. However, external security concerns and threats to the legitimacy of some of these states' regimes (Germany and Japan) also contributed to military investments. The inability to determine the relative explanatory power of each hypothesis implies the need to revise these three propositions and to collect additional data. Table 5.1 summarizes the results of the historical case studies.

Table 5.1

Which Hypotheses Explain Great-Power Military Spending?

Period	France	Germany	Japan	Russia	United States
1870–1890	Ambition	Fear	Fear	Ambition	Ambition
1891–1913	Fear	Ambition, fear, and legitimacy	Ambition and fear	Ambition and fear	Ambition and fear
1919–1939	Fear	Ambition and fear	Ambition, fear and legitimacy	Fear	Fear

FRANCE: COPING WITH GERMANY

For the 69 years following the Franco-Prussian War, French policymakers focused on first reestablishing their nation's place among the great powers and later confronting the potential security threat from

Germany. French actions from 1870 to 1890 provide mild support for the ambition hypothesis. Growth in the French economy heightened its desire for retribution against Germany, while prompting a generation of politicians to enlarge France's colonial holdings. While the French may have craved an opportunity to repay German aggression, they simply lacked the economic and military capabilities to exact revenge in the twenty years following the Franco-Prussian war. Adding to its colonial empire proved a better bet. In subsequent years (1891–1939), fear of German power became the primary motivation behind French foreign policy and the decision to raise military spending.

Military spending: 1870–1890. From 1870 to 1890, French military expenditures followed two patterns. In the first eleven years after the war with Prussia, real French investments in the military grew from $1.3 to $2.3 billion.[2] For the remaining nine years of this era, policymakers in Paris kept military spending constant at around $2.5 billion. Growth in military expenditures correlates with France's pursuit of additional colonies.

Possible explanations. The ambition hypothesis appears to offer the best account of French military spending after the Franco-Prussian War. Growth in French foreign ambitions appears to mirror the growth in the French economy. From 1872 to 1890, real French GDP rose from $54 billion to $75 billion.[3] At the same time, French politicians seemed to see the enlargement of France's colonial empire as a more important goal than overturning the territorial settlement established with the Treaty of Frankfurt in 1871. France joined the scramble for Africa and momentarily put aside aspirations for regaining its lost provinces of Alsace-Lorraine (Taylor, 1954). Policymakers devoted most of France's economic and military resources not to a security competition with Germany but to secure holdings in Algeria and Tunisia. France, which until 1875 had led the continental powers in industrialization,[4] mimicked British efforts to find new markets and raw materials in Africa. France's pursuit of colonies was a search for profit as well as prestige. After the acquisition of Tunis in

---

[2]Military expenditures measured in 1982 U.S. dollars.

[3]Gross domestic product measured in 1982 U.S. dollars.

[4]On the French economy, see Kemp (1969).

1881, the French Prime Minister Léon Gambetta felt bold enough to proclaim that "France is becoming a great power again."[5]

Military spending: 1891–1913. In the 23 years before World War I, French military expenditures mostly varied with the growing German security threat. From 1890 to 1901, French decisionmakers increased military spending slightly from $2.4 billion to $2.9 billion. A two-year lull in French economic growth pushed military expenditures from $2.9 billion in 1901 to less than $2.5 billion in 1904. In the following years, a more hostile German foreign policy persuaded France to invest more in its military. The most extreme increase in military expenditures occurred during the period from 1910 to 1913. During those years, French policymakers raised military spending from $2.8 billion to $3.6 billion.

Possible explanations. In the two decades before the Great War, Germany's enhanced material capabilities and belligerent foreign policy increased both French security anxieties and military expenditures. For French policymakers, security concerns replaced colonial ambitions. As Premier Georges Clemenceau put it, "under all circumstances, the vital questions will be settled for us on the frontier of the Vosges; the rest is nothing but accessory."[6] The leaders of the Third Republic began to focus their attention on the continent as German economic might prompted a more assertive diplomacy from Berlin. Accordingly, French behavior provides evidence for the fear hypothesis.

France's perception of a German threat rested on three factors. First, Germany possessed greater economic and military capabilities than France. The disparity between French and German economic power grew larger from 1891 to 1913. For example, by 1910 Germany produced steel at a rate six times faster than France and consumed three times more energy than its neighbor to the west (Kennedy, 1987, pp. 200–201). In 1913, French gross national product only amounted to 55 percent of German GDP (Bairoch, 1982, p. 291). Demographics also put the French at a disadvantage. While the German population increased by 18 million from 1890 to 1914, France saw its population

---

[5]Quoted in Brunschwig (1964, p. 80).

[6]Quoted in Kupchan (1994, p. 208).

grow by only one million in the same period (Spengler, 1951, pp. 403–416; Kennedy, 1987, p. 223). To maintain an army of equal size, policymakers adopted a policy of universal conscription that required three years of service. In peacetime, France always maintained a larger army than Germany. However, France could only draw upon a manpower pool of five million during a conflict, while Germany could count on 10 million eligible men to fill the ranks of its armed forces. Moreover, the German army possessed significant material and organizational advantages over the French military.[7]

Second, Berlin's hostile foreign policy added to the perception of threat in Paris. Under the guidance of Chancellor Bernhard von Bülow, Germany pursued *Weltpolitik*, or world policy, and began to encroach on France's colonial interests. A sizable increase in the German navy implied that Berlin sought to turn back some of France's gains in Africa and challenge the British for maritime supremacy. Twice, in 1905 and 1911, Germany challenged French policy in Morocco (Bridge and Bullen, 1980, pp. 143–162). Later, *Weltpolitik* emphasized German ambitions for territory in Central Europe. Germany's support for Austria in the Balkans brought it into several diplomatic crises with Russia, France's principal ally. Eventually, a dispute in the Balkans would spark World War I.

Third, France worried about the reliability of its allies. While France and its partners in the Triple Entente could threaten Germany with a war on multiple fronts, Paris feared abandonment from its friends in London and St. Petersburg. Before the turn of the century, French policymakers realized they could not face Germany alone and decided to tie French security to Russia. French and Russian diplomats believed the prospect of a two-front war would deter Germany from aggression. Unfortunately for the new anti-German alliance, defeat at the hands of the Japanese in 1905 and a revolution in the same year all but knocked Russia from the European balance of power. Uncertain about Russia and still fearful of Germany, French diplomats turned their attention to repairing relations with their former colonial rival Britain. But as London and Paris discussed how to deal with the German threat, French politicians nevertheless felt uneasy

---

[7]On the disadvantages faced by the French Army, see Porch (1981).

about the prospects of the British army coming to their aid in the event of war.[8]

Military spending: 1919–1939. In the 1920s and early 1930s, French military expenditures fluctuated considerably, from under $2 billlion to as high as $7.5 billion during the 20-year period. The volatility of French military investments reflected three factors: changing economic conditions, the construction of the Maginot Line, and France's occupation of the Ruhr in 1923. However, the rise in military spending from 1933 to 1939, the years of German rearmament, signifies a striking trend. In those six years, French decisionmakers almost doubled their expenditures on the military from $4.3 billion to $7.5 billion.

Possible explanations. During the interwar years, France again found itself preoccupied with the security threat posed by Germany. At the Versailles peace conference, Marshal Ferdinand Foch predicted, "This is not peace. It is an armistice for 20 years."[9] Fear of German economic and military capabilities, coupled with Adolf Hitler's calls to expand his country's borders to incorporate some of Germany's ethnic brethren, motivated France to invest more in its armed forces. As in the years preceding World War I, France suffered from a scarcity of reliable allies to help defend it against a neighbor growing more powerful every year. Moreover, the French leadership realized that Germany harbored deep resentments over its treatment by the Allies, and particularly France, under the Treaty of Versailles.

Despite French efforts to keep its former adversary down, Germany remained the most economically powerful country in Europe. Along several dimensions, the German economy overshadowed its French counterpart. German GDP in 1926 exceeded French GDP by almost $50 billion, a margin of superiority that Germany would enlarge over the next 11 years. French GDP fell to half the size of German GDP by 1935.[10] Even after World War I, Germany consumed twice as much energy as France. Following the downturn of the early 1930s, France

---

[8]For a description of alliance dynamics before World War I, see Joll (1984, pp. 42–68).

[9]Quoted in Bell (1986, p. 16).

[10]These comparisons are heavily influenced by exchange rate movements and choice of deflator.

produced only one-fifth the amount of steel as Germany.[11] Further, the French economy did not recover from the worldwide depression quickly. Perhaps the most disturbing indicator of French economic vulnerabilities came in 1938. In that year, France's national income was 18 percent less than it had been in 1929 (Kennedy, 1987, p. 311).[12]

German military power also represented a formidable threat to French security. In the years following the Versailles settlement, France possessed the second-largest army in Europe.[13] Hitler's rise to power in Germany culminated in the beginning of a rearmament campaign. While French military spending grew from $4.3 billion in 1933 to $6.8 billion in 1938, it could not keep pace with the German buildup. In contrast, German military expenditures would rise from $3.7 billion to $55 billion in the same period. Except for the Soviet Union, Germany spent at least seven times more than any other great power of the era (Kennedy, 1987, p. 296).

To counter the threat from Germany prior to World War I, France crafted alliances first with Russia and later with Britain. Two factors prevented a similar arrangement before World War II. While an alliance remained possible with Britain, ideology and territorial disagreements separated France from Russia. The Soviet leadership in Moscow had more in common with Berlin than with Paris: Germany and Russia could agree that the settlement after World War I had deprived both countries of valuable territory. Therefore, in an effort to contain German power, France entered into a series of bilateral agreements with the newly created states of Eastern Europe from 1924 to 1927, known as the Little Entente. The Allies created these countries out of territory from the former German and Russian Empires. Not only did France and the Soviet Union differ over the territorial settlements of the Versailles agreement, but they also remained ideologically hostile to one another. French policymakers preferred to ally with a semi-democratic Poland in efforts to counter Nazi

---

[11]Figures for energy production and steel production come from Singer and Small (1993).

[12]Again, exchange rate movements are important here. In 1982 dollars, the large decline in French national income came between 1934 and 1938.

[13]The largest European fighting force belonged to the Soviet Union (Gooch, 1980, pp. 191–195).

Germany and Communist Russia. Similarly, Stalin viewed France suspiciously since it represented a member of the allied coalition that had intervened militarily during the Russian civil war.

Finally, Hitler's aggressive foreign policy frightened France. Beginning with the decision to no longer comply with the Versailles limitations on German armaments, Hitler's diplomacy toward Britain and France became more aggressive in its pursuit of additional territory. Although it had conducted clandestine military training missions with the Soviet Union in defiance of the postwar settlement, the Weimar government typically chose to maintain the territorial status quo.[14] But a series of events would solidify Hitler's aggressive image in the mind of French policymakers. By the winter of 1939, Hitler led Germany to revitalize its military, to remilitarize the Rhineland, to incorporate Austria, and to annex the remainder of Czechoslovakia.[15]

GERMANY: TWO FAILED BIDS FOR EUROPEAN HEGEMONY

Two different trends in foreign policy drove German military expenditures from 1870 to 1939. First, in the 20 years following its stunning victory in the Franco-Prussian War, Germany sought to maintain the territorial status quo against a possibly irredentist France. Bismarck's creation of a series of alliances to counter the possibility of a two-front war against France and Russia are consistent with the fear hypothesis. The second trend in German foreign policy occurred before both World Wars. In these years, German military expenditures reflected both a desire for continental expansion and an attempt to bolster its security against the encircling alliances Bismarck worked hard to prevent.

Military expenditures: 1870–1890. After its war with France, German policymakers increased military spending at a steady rate. Between 1872 and 1886, German investment in its armed forces doubled from $765 million to $1.4 billion. In this period, Germany's

[14]On the differences between the foreign policies of the Weimar Republic and Nazi Germany, see Weinberg (1970).

[15]For a good summary of French diplomacy before World War II, see Adamthwaite (1977).

incremental growth in military expenditures mirrored the spending of the other European great powers. A sharp rise in German expenditures from 1886 to 1887 grew out of a brief episode of colonization in Southwest Africa. For the last three years of Bismarck's reign as German chancellor, however, military spending declined to the benign levels of the previous years.

Possible explanations. Except for a brief two-year sprint to establish a colony in Southwest Africa, the fear hypothesis offers the best explanation for the pattern in German military spending from 1870 to 1890. Although Germany experienced considerable economic growth in this 20-year period, Bismarck worked hard to contain the ambitions of other German military leaders and politicians for expansion (von Eyck, 1958). German GDP increased from $55 billion to $83 billion from 1870 to 1890. However, Germany did not demonstrate the same drive for expansion that it would before World War I. For Bismarck, preserving the territorial settlement embedded in the Treaty of Frankfurt served Germany's interests.

To maintain the German gains won in the Franco-Prussian War, Bismarck pursued two primary goals (Bridge and Bullen, 1980, pp. 112–124). First, he sought to bolster Germany's image as a secure and, more important, satisfied state. The German victory over France had created a new and powerful nation in the center of Europe. Britain as well as France worried that unification would permit Germany to further adjust the European balance of power against it. These concerns were justified. First, Germany possessed great potential economic power. In 1870, Germany already possessed 13 percent of the world's industrial production (Kennedy, 1987, p. 192). Moreover, with its victories at Sadowa and Sedan, Germany and its Prussian-led General Staff had already demonstrated that it possessed a military that was not only well armed but skilled. Superior economic and military capabilities could keep Germany secure as long as its leaders took precautions to avoid acting in ways that might provoke a coalition of the great powers to form against it. To create the perception of a benign Germany, Bismarck set out to serve as Europe's "honest broker" (Taylor, 1954, pp. 180–225). After the Franco-Prussian War, the center of gravity in European politics had shifted from Paris to Berlin and Bismarck used that to his advantage. During his tenure as chancellor, Berlin hosted a series of meetings to resolve disputes arising out of the scramble for Africa.

Bismarck's second aim was to bolster Germany's security by forging a network of European alliances (Taylor, 1967, pp. 158–193). The German chancellor rightly feared that France and Russia might find in one another perfect allies to counter German power. Bismarck's strategy contained two tenuous elements: allying Germany with the Austro-Hungarian Empire, while maintaining good relations with the Russian Empire. The decision to tie German security to Austria rested in large part on economic ties and a mutual interest in preventing Russian expansion into the Balkans (Calleo, 1978, p. 18). As tricky as it seemed, Bismarck endeavored to prevent conflict between Austria and Russia. The German chancellor already knew he would have to side with his southern neighbor in such a situation, and Germany's choice would likely drive Russia into the arms of France. To reduce the possibility of that unhappy occurrence, Bismarck created the Three Emperors League, an alliance based on the common conservative political ideologies of Hohenzollern, Habsburg, and Romanov dynasties. Shared notions of domestic politics, however, could not keep Austria and Russia from clashing over the Balkans. As a result, Bismarck moved Germany closer to Austria through the formation of the Dual Alliance of 1878. This decision would complicate the strategic considerations of future German policymakers (Kaiser, 1983).

Military spending: 1891–1913. Military spending in Germany averaged $2.4 billion from 1891 to 1898, a lower level of spending than undertaken by the French government at the time. From 1898 to 1913, German decisionmakers allocated more funding to the military. A large portion of this increase stemmed from the decision to create a navy capable of threatening Britain's primacy of the seas. Germany's concerted naval build up pushed its military expenditures past France in 1902. By 1913, Germany invested $4.8 billion in its armed forces, surpassing all of the great powers in military spending.

Possible explanations. All three hypotheses provide explanations for the rapid increase in German military expenditures. First, evidence exists to support the ambition hypothesis. German industrial capacity almost doubled from 1891 to 1913. A sharp rise in GDP in 1903 marked a significant increase in Germany's relative economic power. In that year, Germany passed all of the great powers, except for the United States, on most measures of industrial capability (Kennedy, 1987, pp. 209–210). Germany's ambitions began to match its new economic prominence. Under the leadership of Kaiser Wilhelm II and his new chancellor, Bernhard von Bülow, Germany adopted its *Weltpolitik*. The goal of this new foreign policy rested on the pursuit of colonies in Africa and Asia. Continued economic growth, so the argument went, required greater access to raw materials (Kaiser, 1983). Germany planned to follow Britain on the path to further economic growth by expanding its markets abroad. At the same time, German planners hoped its added naval presence would deter Britain from interfering with its global ambitions (Rohl, 1967, pp. 156–175). A final element of *Weltpolitik* was an aggressive diplomacy based on the belief that threats to use force would accomplish more than cooperation (Geiss, 1976).

Second, in accordance with the fear hypothesis, Germany reacted to legitimate security threats. Italy and the sickly Austro-Hungarian Empire remained Germany's only allies in this period, while it found itself faced with the possibility of a two-front war (Joll, 1984, pp. 42–69). Initially, Germany had only to worry about the anti-German coalition formed by France and Russia in 1893. But Britain's decision to enter the Franco-Russian entente in 1907 raised the level of anxiety in Berlin (Keylor, 1984, p. 48). The economic and military capabilities of these three countries exceeded the capabilities of Germany and its lackluster allies (Kennedy, 1987, pp. 256–260). Moreover, Berlin's insecurities also centered on the conviction that the other great powers might corner existing markets for overseas trade. Finally, the German political leadership feared that their country's relative military power would begin to decline in the face of the French and Russian decisions to increase their standing armies (Fischer, 1974, 1975).

Third, the kaiser's government also used foreign policy as a tool to deflect attention from its domestic failures (Mayer, 1967, p. 297; Jarausch, 1973; Snyder, 1991).[16] The legitimacy hypothesis predicts the German regime would exaggerate international security threats and adopt an aggressive style of diplomacy to garner political support. Economic modernization in Germany had created ever-widening social chasms between a large middle class calling for

---

[16]For a discussion of the role of interest groups in German foreign policy, see Hull (1982).

greater political liberalization and the conservative interest groups that already dominated the government (Rich, 1992). While the elected members of the Reichstag controlled the government's finances, the kaiser appointed the prime minister and his cabinet members without interference from his parliament. Similarly, the military largely evaded control by civilians in government (Mommsen, 1973).

The German leadership answered the calls by social democrats for greater political liberalization in two ways. Beginning with Bismarck, the conservative German government transformed the social democrats into a movement better characterized as the "loyal opposition" than a real threat to the regime. Policies guaranteeing health insurance and worker's rights took significant pressure off the kaiser and his government. Second, German politicians like von Bülow and Theobald Bethmann-Hollweg recognized that diplomatic successes abroad could bolster their power at home. Part of this strategy involved inculcating the German populace with nationalist rhetoric and notions of Social Darwinism (Ritter, 1969–1973, vol. 2). "Survival of the fittest" as a theme for international politics found adherents in Germany as well as in many other European states. Although historians seem to disagree how successful German policymakers and their allies among different interest groups were in their ability to convince the German public that an arms race was necessary, domestic political considerations alone probably did not fuel military spending. More likely, it seems that domestic struggles prompted government officials to exaggerate both German ambitions and insecurities.

Military spending: 1919–1939. The end of World War I prompted a huge decrease in German military spending. From 1919 to 1933, Germany would comply with the provisions of the Versailles Treaty and maintain an army of no more than 100,000 men. An exception to this trend occurred in 1923. In that year, Britain and France permitted Germany to procure a large police force to combat domestic threats against the Weimar Republic. The most notable shift in military expenditures transpired after Adolf Hitler's rise to power in 1933. Five years later, German military expenditures increased by a factor of 18, from $3.7 billion to almost $55 billion.

Possible explanations. Consistent with the ambition hypothesis, German ambitions appeared to grow along with its economy. While Germany possessed one of the most powerful economies of the 1920s, war reparations and a worldwide economic downturn dampened its industrial growth. By the mid-1930s, however, Germany began to experience a rapid economic recovery. Under the guidance of the National Socialist government, German GDP doubled from 1932 to 1937.[17] Concurrently, Germany began to abrogate portions of the Versailles Treaty. After three years in power, Hitler announced the return of military conscription in Germany, a clear violation of the Versailles settlement (Taylor, 1963). To return Germany to its status as a great power, Hitler planned to revamp his country's military forces (Bell, 1986, pp. 77–97). Commenting on the reaction to Germany's rearmament Hitler noted, "A balance of power had been established without Germany's participation. This balance is being disturbed by Germany claiming her vital rights and her reappearance in the circle of the great powers."[18]

The fear hypothesis offers an alternative account of Hitler's rearmament campaign. Hitler's Germany faced many of the same security threats it faced in the previous period. To the west, Britain and France represented guardians of the Versailles settlement. Together, these allies possessed greater military capabilities than Germany, and by 1936, they had responded to Hitler's rearmament drive with increases in their own military expenditures (Ross, 1983, pp. 90–108). To the east, Germany faced a corridor of states that had been created out of its former territory and remnants of the Habsburg and Romanov Empires. Four of these states, Czechoslovakia, Hungary, Poland, and Yugoslavia, had aligned with France, Germany's principal adversary (Keylor, 1984, pp. 57–59). Further east, German planners had to consider the security threat from a Soviet Union with an enormous population, possessing an inimical political ideology, that had experienced rapid rates of industrialization in the 1930s.

Not only did Hitler and his strategists have to contend with the encirclement of hostile states, but they also had to consider how Ger-

---

[17]It is impossible to say definitively, however, whether Germany's economic growth during this period drove increases in military expenditures or vice versa.

[18]Quoted in Schweller (1998, p. 107).

many would secure raw material for its growing economy and population (Kaiser, 1980). This was a recurring theme in German foreign policy. At the turn of the century, German policymakers worried about how they would gain access to international markets and find the necessary resources to fuel their industrial economy. The situation in the 1930s differed in one important aspect: Germany could no longer rely on the valuable iron-ore-rich provinces of Alsace-Lorraine. Hitler devised his policy of *Lebensraumpolitik* to solve Germany's resource difficulties. Unlike Kaiser Wilhelm II, Hitler wanted Germany to pursue territory in Europe in lieu of colonies in Africa. Early in his political career he argued, "For Germany . . . the only possibility of carrying out a sound territorial policy was to be found in the acquisition of new soil in Europe proper."[19] In the short term, Hitler planned to rebuild the Germany military and seize by force the resources necessary for long-term economic growth.

JAPAN: MILITARY GOVERNMENTS AND THE SEARCH FOR AUTARKY

The pattern of Japanese military expenditures reflects territorial expansion motivated by rapid rates of economic growth, insecurity bred from the looming presence of the European great powers, and the domestic political struggles between civilian and military leaders. In this way, Japanese history echoes many of the same themes found in German history. As such, we find support for all three hypotheses at different periods of Japanese history. Initially, fear of succumbing to the colonial feeding frenzy that had victimized China prompted Japanese leaders to embark on significant internal political and economic reforms. Eventually, economic modernization as well as the need for natural resources to sustain a growing industrial capacity would engender Japanese colonial ambitions. Before World War II, Japan's military leaders would take advantage of adverse economic conditions to seize control of the government and adopt a foreign policy designed to resolve their country's resource deficiencies through conquest.

---

[19]Quoted in Schweller (1998), p. 107.

Military spending: 1870–1890. For centuries a decentralized oligarchy of territorial landlords (*daimyo*) and an aristocratic caste of warriors (*samurai*) ruled the island nation of Japan. This changed in 1868 when a group of dynamic political elites restored power to the emperor and created a powerful central government in an event known as the Meiji Restoration. An imperial army replaced the *samurai* and the emperor's bureaucracy reduced the political influence of the *daimyo*. The desire to transform Japan into a modern great power motivated these ambitious reformers. Government leaders modeled their economy after the United States, embraced the tenets of the British political system, and imitated the highly efficient Prussian military (Keylor, 1984, p. 14). The steady growth in Japanese military expenditures from 1870 to 1890 reflects the success of the Meiji reformers. Investments in the Japanese military quickly rose to $100 million and remained at that level for fifteen years. As the government embarked on a new modernization program from 1885 to 1890, investments in the military nearly doubled.

Possible explanations. In part, Japanese military spending after the Meiji Restoration stemmed from its economic takeoff. Driven by domestic reforms, Japan's industrial capacity more than doubled from 1875 to 1890. Its annual GDP rose from $6 billion to slightly more than $14 billion. However, while the trend in military expenditures mirrored the growth in the Japanese economy, this pattern does not provide conclusive support for the ambition hypothesis. In particular, growth in the Japanese economy did not spark an expansionist foreign policy. Insecurity appears to have been the primary motivation for the Meiji Restoration, and these fears provided the incentive for the subsequent modernization of the Japanese military.

The Meiji leadership faced at least two security problems. These concerns, and not unbridled ambitions, drove policymakers to increase military spending. First, policymakers worried that Japan would fall victim to the colonial ambitions of the great powers (Beasley, 1972, p. 11). To the west, the European powers had already begun extracting concessions from China. In 1853, the United States sent Commodore Matthew Perry to forcefully persuade the Japanese to allow foreign trade. The desire to avoid China's fate prompted the Meiji elites to implement the necessary economic and political changes that would make Japan into a modern industrial power. "Rich country; strong army," became the slogan of Japan's reformers.[20] Because Japan lacked allies to form an alliance against the European colonizers, the Japanese government believed internal reform provided the best defense against European imperial designs.

Second, Japanese policymakers began to worry that Japan, as an island nation lacking arable land, could not sustain long-term industrialization. Not only did Japan suffer from a shortage of land to produce agricultural products, but the country faced a shortage of raw materials needed to fuel its economic expansion (Kobayashi, 1922). During the 1880s, a sharp rise in its population compounded Japan's resource problems. Already afraid of foreign invasion, the Japanese leadership began to search for colonies of its own (Keylor, 1984, pp. 15–16). To fend off the encroachments of the European powers, Japan needed to continue its economic modernization. Government officials considered a formidable military necessary for defense and for the eventual seizure of raw materials outside of Japan (Beasley, 1987, Chaps. 4–7).

Military spending: 1891–1913. Efforts at territorial expansion drove Japanese military spending in this period. A war with China (1894–1895) precipitated a sharp fourfold increase in Japanese military expenditures from $242 million in 1891 to $862 million in 1897. The Japanese government kept its investments in the military at this level until the years preceding conflict with Russia. A confrontation with the Russian Empire over Korea pushed military spending to $4.2 billion. After inflicting a severe defeat on the Russian army and securing its hold over the Korean peninsula, Japan lowered its spending on the armed forces to near $1.2 billion annually. Japanese policymakers sustained this level of military spending through World War I.

Possible explanations. This period of Japanese history supports the ambition hypothesis. Greater economic growth spurred greater levels of military spending as well as a more ambitious foreign policy. From 1891 to 1913, Japan experienced rapid rates of economic expansion. Japanese GDP almost doubled from $14 billion in 1891 to $25 billion by the eve of World War I. Concurrently, the government increased military spending from $259 million to $1 billion, almost a fourfold rise in funding. While the Japanese economy grew at a brisk

---

[20]Quoted in Barnhart (1987).

pace, the country's foreign policy became more energetic (Jensen, 1984). The war with China secured Japanese colonies in Taiwan and eventually Korea. To preserve their gains in Korea, Japanese officials decided in 1904 to dislodge Russia from Manchuria. The Japanese military victories over Russia signaled the arrival of Japan as a great power. While Japan lost the peace to Russia at the Portsmouth Conference, it did manage to solidify its position in Korea and increase its influence in Manchuria (Duus, 1976, pp. 52–78).

The fear hypothesis can also explain Japanese foreign policy. Although Japan's economic performance appeared to have motivated territorial expansion, security concerns also played a role in its aggressive designs and the growth in its military expenditures. The resource concerns of the earlier period continued to plague Japanese policymakers. To sustain their country's economic expansion, Japan's leaders needed additional sources of raw materials to reduce its dependence on imports. Manchuria's rich deposits of iron ore proved an inviting target for bolstering Japanese steel production. A growing population also created pressures on already strained food production. Policymakers calculated that the acquisition of colonies would provide an outlet for emigration as well as the opportunity to increase the amount of arable land for producing food that Japan desperately needed.[21]

In addition to shortages of raw materials, Japanese decisionmakers also worried about the security threats from their powerful American and Russian rivals.[22] To the west, Russian expansion into Asia had resulted in the construction of the Trans-Siberian railway. The Japanese leadership correctly concluded that Russia aspired to seize control of Manchuria and its supply of raw materials. To the east, the United States had begun to increase the size of its naval forces and had started construction of the Panama Canal. Relations between Tokyo and Washington took a turn for the worse when American policymakers decided to restrict Japanese immigration to the United States (Keylor, 1994, pp. 19–23). For the Japanese leadership, these limitations smacked of racism and would serve as cornerstone for a worsening of relations in the decades to come.

---

[21]On Japan's shortage of resources, see Kennedy (1987, pp. 300–301).

[22]Japanese fears of Russia during this period are described in Crowley (1966).

Military spending: 1919–1939. Japanese military spending remained close to $1.8 billion annually from 1919 to 1935. The emergence of a more democratic regime in Japan explains part of this trend. Political reforms implemented by the oligarchs of the Meiji Restoration had liberalized Japan's political system and produced the era of the Taisho democrats, named after the emperor (Yoshihito) who ruled at the time. These parliamentarians actively curbed the military's tendency to exaggerate international security threats for the purpose of territorial expansion. While still acknowledging the need for new external sources of natural resources, the Taisho leadership managed to maintain low levels of military spending and improve relations with the other great powers. A decline in worldwide economic conditions as well as Japan's own agricultural problems put an end to the Taisho regime. Military leaders slowly seized control of the Japanese government and embarked on an ambitious campaign of expansion that began with the annexation of Manchuria in 1931. In a dramatic effort to finally achieve autarky, Japan again invaded China in 1937, sparking a sixfold increase in military spending.

Possible explanations. Prior to World War II, the fear and legitimacy hypotheses provide the best explanations for the patterns in Japanese military spending. In this period, Japan's foreign policy is constrained by two factors: a growing belief that autarky is necessary for the country's survival would dovetail with the rise of militarism. Decisionmakers not only confronted the prospect of greater and greater Soviet military capabilities, but they also faced immediate difficulties in the form of shortages of arable land, petroleum, and rubber products. At the same time, a military-dominated government in Tokyo would exploit these anxieties to pursue territorial expansion in East Asia. From the military's perspective, creating a Japanese empire would solve the country's resource problems as well as bolster their political position at home. While Japanese behavior in the era seems to fit the fear and legitimacy hypotheses best, we also find mild support for the ambition hypothesis. As limited evidence for this line of argument, we note the correlation between the considerable growth in Japanese economic output from 1934 to 1939 and an aggressive foreign policy culminating in Japan's efforts to create a regional co-prosperity sphere.

As in previous years, Japanese decisionmakers believed three factors contributed to Japan's international insecurity. First, the growth in Russian economic and military capabilities that resulted from Stalin's industrialization policies engendered anxiety in Tokyo (Barnhart, 1981). Japan had sought to protect its holdings in Manchuria and northeast China by occupying Siberia in 1918. However, in 1921, the Japanese leadership decided to remove its troops from this area to lower military spending as well as to improve relations with Britain and the United States. Military strategists in Japan worried at the time this move would make Manchuria vulnerable. By 1931, the Soviet Union appeared to have rebounded from its domestic strife. The Japanese military became convinced it needed to prepare for an eventual conflict with the Soviet Union over territory in China. Not only did Japan believe it lacked the industrial resources to fight a prolonged war with the Soviet Union, it also concluded that its military was not up to the cause. The losses suffered by the Kwantung Army during border skirmishes with the Soviet forces in 1938 and 1939 reinforced Japanese perception of inferiority (Barnhart, 1987, pp. 70–92).

Second, the United States also represented a potential security threat to Japan. The U.S. naval presence appeared to Japanese strategists as a potential crimp in their designs for expansion into Southeast Asia. The United States had already established a naval base in the Philippines and maintained the capacity to project power into the Pacific from Hawaii. In addition to the already sizable economic and military power that the United States possessed, Japanese leaders also believed that American policy was intended to check their country's expansion in Asia. The Washington Naval Treaty constrained the expansion of Japanese maritime capabilities while preserving the American advantage in these forces. As a further indicator of the deteriorating relations between the two countries, the Japanese government argued that the United States continued to practice a racist policy of limiting immigration from Japan (Keylor, 1984, pp. 18–19).

Finally, while Japanese strategists perceived security threats from the Soviet Union and the United States, they still faced the problem of resource scarcity. The experience of Germany during World War I taught the Japanese military an important lesson: without its own source of natural resources, Japan would likely lose a protracted conflict against modern industrial powers, such as the Soviet Union and the United States (Keylor, 1984). To the north in China, Japan could procure needed resources like iron ore (Duus, 1976, pp. 23–35). To the south, Japan could secure much needed rubber and petroleum. As in previous years, growth in the Japanese population created a demand for more food and more arable land (Sagan, 1988, pp. 323–352).

While threats to Japan's security existed, the military's control of the government also explains the country's expansionist foreign policy as well as the rapid rise of military expenditures. The Taisho democrats lost their hold of the government when the Japanese economy soured as a result of agricultural failures and the Great Depression (Patrick, 1971). Military leaders blamed Japan's economic problems on a liberal trade policy. Military leaders also used foreign threats to undermine the Taisho government. In 1931, officers of the Japanese Kwantung Army destroyed a segment of the Manchurian railway in Mukden and blamed the incident on China. This event provided the Japanese military with a pretext for the annexation of Manchuria. These actions in China also boosted the popularity of the Japanese military at the expense of more liberal politicians (Barnhart, 1981, pp. 70–92).

Eventually by the mid-1930s, members of the Japanese Army held many of the major positions in government. Japan's military leadership allied itself with the remaining *daimyo* landlords as well as the small coterie of industrialists known as the *zaibatsu*. All three of these groups would profit from an expansionist foreign policy and they actively cultivated a sense of insecurity in Japan to justify such a policy (Snyder, 1991, pp. 112–152). Moreover, the perception of external security threats allowed the military government to retain its legitimacy. In the years preceding its second war with China in 1937, the Japanese leadership garnered support for expansion in two ways. As one part of their strategy, policymakers used nationalist rhetoric to defend their pursuit of economic self-sufficiency through conquest. The other facet of this strategy involved convincing the population that this was a necessary course of action and only the military could complete the task. In the words of one scholar, "[T]he military and bureaucratic elites were able to persuade many of their counterparts in other elites and much of the populace that Japan had entered a period of national crisis in her foreign and domestic affairs, which required an application of military and bureaucratic expertise other parties could not provide."[23]

Although the fear and legitimacy hypotheses offer the most convincing accounts of Japanese foreign policy during this era, there is reason to believe that the ambition hypothesis can also shed light on this period. From 1934 to 1938, Japan experienced a sizeable increase in its industrial output. Japanese GDP during this time grew from $30 billion to $55 billion, almost doubling in eight years. Japan's growth spurt also appeared to spur the country's ambitions. As the nation's economic capacity began to increase, so did its desire for additional territory. Not only did Japan consolidate its hold over Manchuria in these years, it also undertook what would ultimately become an ill-fated campaign to seize the rest of China.

RUSSIA: INTERNATIONAL TROUBLES AND DOMESTIC STRUGGLES

From 1870 to 1939, Russian military expenditures were driven by expansion at the expense of weak neighbors and fear of a powerful Germany. Under the leadership of Tsar Alexander II, Russia enlarged its borders through a war with Turkey and increased its territories in the Far East. While the ambition hypothesis explains the first two decades of Russian behavior, security concerns fostered military spending in subsequent periods. Russia's desire for territorial aggrandizement died with its defeat at the hands of Japan in 1905 and the growing German threat in central Europe. Before World War I, Russian policymakers raised military spending to deter German aggression and to bolster the credibility of their commitments in the Balkans. The strain of war unleashed a revolution and civil war that toppled Russia's tsarist regime. Vladimir Lenin and his Bolshevik revolutionaries seized control of the Russian Empire and established the Soviet Union. In later years, ideological differences isolated Russia from its traditional anti-German allies and prompted Stalin to raise military spending as a matter of self-help.

Military spending: 1870–1890. Improvements in the Russian economy prompted a doubling of military expenditures from 1870 to

---

[23]Gordon Berger, as quoted in Snyder (1991, p. 146).

1890. The reforms undertaken by Tsar Alexander II to push his empire into the industrial era spurred growth in the stagnant Russian economy. Repressive political institutions as well as the earlier Crimean War had stunted industrialization efforts in Russia (de Grunwald, 1954). As the economy began to show signs of life, St. Petersburg allocated more funds for its armed forces.[24] Except for a sharp increase during the Russo-Turkish War (1877–1878), military spending steadily climbed to $2 billion by 1890.

Possible explanations. The ambition hypothesis provides the most accurate insights into Russian behavior during this era. Impressive growth in Russia's industrial capacity fed the foreign ambitions of its policymakers in St. Petersburg. In the 20-year period discussed here, the Russian Empire experienced a tenfold increase in energy consumption.[25] Railway construction and the liberation of the serfs represented only a few of the reforms Alexander II implemented to spur this economic performance (Crankshaw, 1976, pp. 111–122, and Saunders, 1992, p. 191). Although Russia still failed to match the other great powers in industrial capabilities, this largely agrarian state still made enough economic progress in these two decades to pursue a fairly ambitious foreign policy.

Alexander II and his advisors set out to erase the setbacks Russia suffered during the Crimean War (Jelavich, 1974). Although Russia could not expand westward, it felt capable of acquiring more territory from the disintegrating Ottoman Empire. A brief war with the Ottomans from 1877 to 1878 enlarged Russia's southern borders and increased its influence in the Balkans (Rich, 1992, pp. 307–312). A few years later, St. Petersburg's relations with London soured over the Far East. British officials grew alarmed by the steady Russian advance into central Asia. Fear arose in the British Empire that Russia would threaten India. Britain believed an agreement signed in 1873 to maintain current borders in the region would halt Russia's drive toward Afghanistan and Persia. Most Russian policymakers discounted this treaty, and they eventually pushed their country's frontiers toward the Afghan city of Penjedh by 1885. Britain responded to this last move by threatening Russia with war. Even

---

[24]For a useful discussion of the Russian economy, see Gerschenkron (1962).

[25]We use the energy production data provided by Singer and Small (1993).

though Britain could not muster enough allies to mount another Crimean campaign against Russia, the tsar calculated that pursuing his Far East policy was not worth risking another costly European conflict.[26]

Military spending: 1891–1913. In the fifteen years prior to World War I, Russian military expenditures climbed from $3 billion to $4.6 billion annually. A disastrous war with Japan (1904–1905) accounts for a large part of the increase in economic resources devoted to the military, propelling Russia to a new high of almost $11 billion in 1905. However, Russia's first revolution, in 1905, crippled the economy and contributed to a reduction in military expenditures. As political stability returned, Russia's industrial growth rebounded. The adroit leadership of the prime minister, Piotr Stolypin, provided a stable political environment under Tsar Nicholas II for Russia to continue its march to the industrial era (Kemp, 1969, pp. 114–148). While still far behind most of its peer competitors, the Russian Empire of 1913 seemed destined to join the ranks of Europe's economic great powers (Kennedy, 1987, pp. 232–241).

Possible explanations. We find support for both the ambition and fear hypotheses in this era of Russian foreign policy. The ambition hypothesis offers the best insights into Russian territorial ambitions in the Far East. Grateful for St. Petersburg's security commitment to France, Paris contributed loans for Russia's strong economic expansion (Taylor, 1954, pp. 286–294). Russian energy consumption tripled in the fifteen years before the Russo-Japanese War. Foreign investment permitted Tsar Alexander III to begin the construction of the Trans-Siberian Railway, thereby strengthening the connection between the eastern and western halves of the empire when it was completed in 1904. Russia had already established a military presence in Manchuria and hoped to extract its large reserve of iron ore. Unfortunately for Russia, Japanese policymakers began to feel that Russia's enlarged presence in the Far East threatened Japan's hold on the Korean peninsula. Japan's attack on Port Arthur (now Lushun, China) in 1904 marked the beginning of a war with Russia. One year later, in spite of the losses suffered by its military at the

[26]Our description of the Anglo-Russian disputes in central Asia relies on Bridge and Bullen (1980, p. 131–132).

hands of the Japanese, Russia's diplomats managed to secure a territorial stalemate at the Portsmouth conference. The military loss to Japan and subsequent revolution in 1905 forced Tsar Nicholas II to place Russia's Asian ambitions aside.

While the ambition hypothesis explains St. Petersburg's behavior before the Russo-Japanese War, Russian foreign policy in the remaining years of the Romanov dynasty provides evidence for the fear hypothesis. Germany's economic and military capabilities forced Russian policymakers to turn their attention from Asia to central Europe. Two factors contributed to Russian insecurities. First, Germany surpassed Russia on most indicators of aggregate economic capability (Joll, 1984, pp. 146–170). By the early part of the twentieth century, the German Empire had vaulted ahead of the British as the greatest industrial power of Europe (Kennedy, 1987, p. 231). To counter German economic strength, Russia could draw on a vast population to field a significantly larger army. However, logistical difficulties, a shortage of equipment, and its poor performance against the Japanese army raised doubts about the quality of Russia's armed forces (Stone, 1975).

Second, Germany's alliance with Austria-Hungary threatened Russia's interests in the Balkans. Although Kaiser Wilhelm II tried on several occasions, most notably in 1905, to lure his cousin into a nonaggression pact, the tsar remained committed to the Franco-Russian entente. Turned down by Russia, Germany drew closer to the declining Austro-Hungarian Empire. Citing ethnic bonds, Russia considered itself the guardian of the fledgling Slavic states that sprang from the ailing Ottoman Empire. This commitment ran counter to Austria's desire to enlarge its borders at the expense of these Balkan states (Bridge and Bullen, 1980, pp. 157–167). Twice, Germany successfully used threats of war to deter Russia from opposing Austrian expansion in the region. Russia would ultimately call Germany's bluff in July 1914 (Joll, 1984, pp. 10–38).

Military spending: 1919–1939. War with Germany helped topple Russia's tsarist regime in 1917. A year later, Lenin's Bolsheviks took power in war-weary Russia. A hastily arranged peace settlement with Germany, the Treaty of Brest-Litovsk, allowed Lenin's revolutionary government to consolidate power and transform the Russian Empire into the Soviet Union (Carr, 1953). After surviving a bitter civil war, the new Soviet leadership initiated a series of economic reforms. Stalin's five-year plans helped bring the country's primarily agrarian economy into the industrial age. In conjunction with this improved industrial capacity, Soviet military expenditures swelled from $19 billion in 1932 to $44 billion in 1939.

Possible explanations. This trend in military spending illustrates a common theme in Russian foreign policy: the potential security threat from Germany. The fear hypothesis provides the most persuasive account of Soviet investments in its armed forces during this period. In the 16 years prior to the outbreak of World War II, the Russian economy experienced more than a ninefold increase in energy consumption.[27] Coal consumption grew from 22,000 coal-ton equivalents in 1923 to 179,000 coal-ton equivalents in 1939. While this level of industrialization should have acted as a catalyst for territorial ambitions, the Soviet leadership focused on internal reforms and did not embark on expansion until the first few years of World War II (Ulam, 1974).

For Soviet planners, the German security threat rested on two pillars. Superior German economic and military capabilities represented the most important feature of this potential danger. War reparations and the economic downturn of the early 1930s failed to extinguish Germany's industrial potential. On his ascension to power, Hitler initiated a rearmament campaign that pushed his country out of its economic listlessness. German policymakers translated their economic gains into greater military power (Kennedy, 1987, p. 288), far exceeding the Soviet Union in military spending. From 1933 to 1939, Germany invested twice as much in its armed forces as their Soviet competitors. In addition, because Stalin's purges had depleted the ranks of its officer corps, the Soviet army lacked the capable leadership it needed to counter the traditionally skillful German military (Erickson, 1962).

Moreover, the Soviet Union could not find allies to balance against the German threat. As a resurgent Germany maneuvered to overturn the Versailles settlement, ideological differences separated Russia from its traditional anti-German allies. This time, Communist Russia

---

[27]On these economic developments, see Grossman (1976–1977).

could not rely on a partnership with democratic France to stop German aggression. Rightly or wrongly, France believed that the Soviet Union sought to infect Europe with the virus of revolution.[28] As a barrier to this possibility and as a means to contain Germany, France chose to ally itself with the new states of Eastern Europe. French policymakers preferred to form a coalition with Czechoslovakia, Hungary, Poland, and Yugoslavia, rather than make overtures to Stalinist Russia. Britain held similar reservations about an alliance with the Soviet Union (Bell, 1986, pp. 131, 136).

From the Soviet perspective, Britain and France seemed more like potential enemies than friends. The victorious allies of World War I had demonstrated their hostile intentions by actively supporting tsarist forces during the Russian civil war. This support included military intervention by Britain, Japan, and the United States.[29] Moreover, the Soviet Union viewed the states of the Little Entente as territory carved out of the old Russian Empire by the Versailles agreement (Keylor, 1984, pp. 107–127). Still further, France's decision to ally with Poland, which had used Russia's civil war as a pretext for seizing a significant chunk of the Ukraine, further distanced Paris from Moscow. In short, the growth in German military power and a shortage of allies forced Stalin to invest more of his country's economic resources in the armed forces.

THE UNITED STATES: EXPANSION ON THE CHEAP

The American case is an anomaly because rapid economic growth did not translate into correspondingly higher rates of military expenditures. Certainly, the United States acquired greater international ambitions as a consequence of its expanding industrial capabilities. What separates American behavior from that of the other great powers, however, is not restraint from expansion but the relatively modest amounts of military spending needed to increase U.S. influence in the world. Although the growth in its industrial capacity outpaced all other countries, the United States did not emerge as an important player in international politics until Ger-

---

[28]On these difficulties, see Haslam (1984) and Hochmann (1984).

[29]For a summary of this intervention, see Walt (1995, pp. 129–168).

many appeared on the verge of winning World War I. We find that in the first two periods outlined here, American foreign policy provides evidence for the ambition hypothesis. The United States prospered and consolidated its position as a regional power. Before World War II, the fear hypothesis presents the best predictions of American behavior as the United States increased military spending in response to German and Japanese aggression.

Military spending: 1870–1890. In the two decades after the Civil War, the United States showed signs of its potential economic and military power but failed to realize it. The bitter domestic conflict had delayed the emergence of the United States as a great power (Rich, 1992, pp. 347–348). By most measures, the American military was relatively weaker than its counterparts across the Atlantic. By 1870, however, the United States began to challenge Britain's industrial primacy.[30] American GDP already exceeded the other great powers, and it would eventually surpass Britain as well as Germany in all indicators of industrial capacity. However, even though the United States could marshal impressive economic resources, its military spending from 1870 to 1890 remained much lower when compared to states of a similar industrial ranking. With few exceptions, American policymakers kept military expenditures between $600 million and $700 million from 1870 to 1884. A naval buildup in 1885 marked the beginning of a steady climb in government investments in the armed forces.

Possible explanations. The trend in American military spending provides mild support for the ambition hypothesis. In this 20-year period, the GDP of the United States more than doubled from $76 billion to $183 billion. This economic boom, however, did not translate into higher rates of military expenditures until 1885, when President Grover Cleveland embarked on a campaign to modernize American naval forces (Sprout and Sprout, 1939). Only efforts to contain revolts by American Indians in the unsettled West prompted increased funding for the country's armed forces. Two domestic factors curtailed the expansionist ambitions of American policymakers and kept military expenditures down. First, the United States still

[30]For a description of the American economic takeoff, see Vatter (1975) and the discussion in Kennedy (1987, pp. 242–249).

faced high levels of debt stemming from the Civil War. Second, these American debts created a banking crisis in 1873 that would later become the catalyst for a sharp economic downturn (Zakaria, 1998, pp. 67–81).

In 1885, President Cleveland signaled a change in foreign policy as he initiated a reform of the U.S. Navy. This naval modernization program, which took place over four years, included the construction of 30 different classes of ships (Zakaria, 1998). American officials, such as Secretary of State Thomas Bayard, sought a more offensive naval posture that permitted the United States to project its military power throughout the hemisphere. Improved maritime capabilities would enable the United States to keep pace with the naval forces of the other great powers (Seager, 1953). While American foreign policy remained fairly unambitious from 1870 to 1890, the pursuit of a larger navy offers some evidence for the ambition hypothesis.

Military spending: 1891–1917. Most historians point to the late 1890s as the time when the United States emerged as a great power (Lafeber, 1986). From 1891 to 1913, concurrent with its emergence as one of the most powerful states in international relations, the United States consolidated its primacy in the Western Hemisphere. Isolationist tendencies of previous periods gave way to an ambitious foreign policy based on greater American naval capabilities. These allowed the United States to project its military power into the Caribbean and Central America. Not only did American policymakers finally live up to the declarations of the Monroe Doctrine, they also extended U.S. territorial holdings as far as the Philippines. Nevertheless, while American military expenditures increased during this period of expansion, they remained lower than those of the European great powers. Before the Spanish-American War, spending on American armed forces hovered above $1 billion. After topping $4 billion in 1899, annual American military expenditures averaged $3.3 billion until the onset of World War I, when they rose to over $40 billion in 1918 and almost $71 billion in 1919.

Possible explanations. In contrast to the previous period, American foreign policy from 1891 to 1913 provides stronger evidence for the ambition hypothesis. As part of the continued economic expansion, GDP in the United States grew from $192 billion to $424 billion, a more than twofold increase. American industrial capabilities also improved. By 1897, the United States surpassed all countries in energy consumption as well as iron and steel production, two leading indicators of industrial performance. Military spending mirrored the growth in the U.S. economy. Exempting the war with Spain, American policymakers tripled their investments in their armed forces, an increase from roughly one billion to more than $3 billion. The naval modernization program stretched into 1893 and was responsible for the initial growth in military spending.

As the American economy grew, so did American ambitions. On its way to becoming the dominant power in the region, the United States first sought to displace British influence in Latin America. In 1895, American officials intervened in Britain's border dispute between Venezuela and British Guiana to signal its primacy in the hemisphere (Blake, 1942). With veiled threats of military force, the United States strenuously urged the British to submit the dispute to arbitration. Secretary of State Richard Olney's note to British government summarized the American position: "Today the United States is practically sovereign in this continent, and its fiat is law upon the subjects to which it confines its interposition . . . [its] infinite resources combined with its isolated position render it master of the situation and practically invulnerable as against any or all other powers."[31] Shrewdly, Britain, distracted with the Boer War, decided not to intrude on American interests and allowed the United States to arbitrate the border dispute.

Three years later in 1898, the United States trained its sights on Spain and its remaining American colonies (Lafeber, 1986). Citing the Spanish government's inability to control events in Cuba, the United States sent a sizable naval force to the Caribbean island. The subsequent explosion of the American battleship *USS Maine* served as a pretext for the American declaration of war against Spain. With superior naval forces, the United States inflicted a quick defeat on a very weak Spain. In addition to securing Cuba as a naval base and Puerto Rico as an occupied territory, the United States also captured Spain's Pacific colony of the Philippines.

---

[31]Quoted in Rich (1992).

After the Spanish-American War, the United States became involved in a number of military interventions designed to influence the domestic politics of various Latin American countries (Perkins, 1937). For example, under the guidance of Theodore Roosevelt, the United States precipitated a revolt by Panamanian separatists against Colombia. The creation of the independent state of Panama opened the way for the construction of a U.S.-built canal connecting the Pacific Ocean with the Caribbean Sea (Beale, 1962). Two years later in 1905, Roosevelt sent armed forces into the Dominican Republic to restore order and to preserve American business interests. A series of American military interventions in Nicaragua began in 1912 and lasted until 1924. In 50 years, the United States had established itself as the preeminent economic and military power in the Western Hemisphere.[32]

The patterns of American foreign policy outlined above seem to fit the predictions of the ambition hypothesis: economic growth motivated an expansionist foreign policy. However, the fear hypothesis also sheds some light on American behavior. Separated by two oceans from its nearest peer competitors, the United States could afford to remain outside many of the disputes that afflicted the European great powers. Without significant regional military challengers, the United States was able to establish supremacy in the Western Hemisphere with relative ease. Therefore, from 1870 to 1917, the United States faced little in the way of security threats.

This strategic situation changed in 1917 with the possibility that Germany might become the dominant power in Europe.[33] A revolution in Russia as well as revolts within the French Army appeared to raise the likelihood that Germany would score a decisive military victory (Ross, 1983, pp. 32–36). It seems plausible to argue that the United States decided to enter the war in order to prevent Germany from becoming a European hegemon (Smith, 1965, and Lippmann, 1964). One could argue, therefore, that the increase in American military spending from $3.2 billion in 1916 to $71 billion in 1919, the

---

[32]A good discussion of U.S.-Latin American relations during this era is Bemis (1943).

[33]Preventing the domination of Eurasia by one power has been a common theme in U.S. foreign policy. See, for example, Art (1991). Spykman (1942) outlines the threats to the United States from a Eurasian hegemon.

last year of the war, provides some evidence for the fear hypothesis as well as the ambition hypothesis.

Military spending: 1919–1939. Throughout the 1920s, U.S. military spending hovered around $5 billion, slightly above the prewar level of about $4 billion. Spending actually increased during the deepest years of the Great Depression. Increased tensions in Asia and in Europe in the five years before the outbreak of World War II sparked a more noticeable increase in the level of U.S. military expenditures, from $6.6 billion to $10 billion.

Possible explanations. Unlike the previous two periods of U.S. foreign policy, we find little support for the ambition hypothesis for the period 1919–1939. Instead, we argue that the fear hypothesis provides the best explanation of American military spending.

U.S. GDP managed to increase from roughly $504 billion in 1919 to over $650 billion in 1929. However, the global depression of the early 1930s erased these economic gains, with GDP not regaining its 1929 level until 1939. American military spending remained buoyant during these years of economic turmoil, but while economic contraction did not further sink U.S. military spending below its postwar lows, it did correlate with an American foreign policy that possessed fewer international ambitions (Drummond, 1968). The United States discarded its aggressive foreign policy of the previous period and focused most of its attention on domestic concerns. Wilsonian idealism gave way to a new trend toward isolationism. American diplomacy sought few international entanglements. When the United States did show an interest in international politics, it emphasized disarmament. U.S. peacemaking is demonstrated by American efforts at the Washington naval conferences of 1921–1922 and U.S. influence in crafting the Kellogg-Briand Pact of 1928 (Keylor, 1984).

For most of the 1930s, the United States remained preoccupied with finding ways to alleviate the domestic economic distress caused by the Great Depression. Although geography rendered the United States fairly secure, the resurgent aims of Germany and Japan did catch the attention of U.S. policymakers (Dalleck, 1979). Hitler's rearmament campaign as well as Japanese aggression against China encouraged higher levels of American military spending. One year after Hitler took Germany out of the League of Nations (in 1934), U.S.

military expenditures rose from $5.3 billion to $6.6 billion. By 1939, the United States was devoting $10 billion to its armed forces.[34]

CONCLUSION

The case studies offer mixed support for all three hypotheses. Military expenditures driven by security concerns, or the fear hypothesis, is the most prevalent explanation. That insecurity encouraged great-power military spending makes sense since many of these states experienced rapid rates of economic growth and shared common borders. A neighbor with expanding industrial and military capabilities is likely to appear threatening. However, these five great powers also invested in their armed forces in a manner consistent with the ambition hypothesis. In at least one period, economic modernization engendered ambitious foreign policies. Finally, these cases provide little evidence for the legitimacy hypothesis. While domestic politics always played a role in a government's foreign policy and procurement decisions, we find only two episodes (Germany, 1891–1913; and Japan, 1919–1939) where the dynamics of the legitimacy hypothesis seem to have occurred.

---

[34]For an excellent treatment of the American decision to become involved in World War II, see Heinrichs (1988).

Chapter Six

SHOULD THE UNITED STATES WORRY ABOUT LARGE, FAST-GROWING ECONOMIES?

This report represents an initial investigation into the relationship between economic growth and military expenditures for candidate great powers. On the basis of three hypotheses about that relationship—"ambition," "fear," and "legitimacy"—we have undertaken two types of empirical tests: a statistical analysis of the ambition and fear hypotheses, and historical case studies of all three hypotheses. While our statistical analysis is ambiguous with respect to the ambition and fear hypotheses, the case studies provide some evidence in support of both.

Overall, the evidence offered by this report suggests that large and fast-growing economies are likely to devote an increasing, but not disproportionately increasing, share of their growing national resources to their militaries. Since circa 1870, four of the five great powers we examined increased their military expenditures as they experienced dramatic transformations in economic growth, with significant consequences for international politics. However, the direction of causality between military expenditures and economic growth has not been established, and perhaps more important, the motivations behind military expenditure growth probably include complex combinations of ambition, fear, and to a lesser extent, legitimacy.

The critical question at this juncture, therefore, is whether the United States ought to be concerned about the prospect of increased military expenditures on the part of large and rapidly growing economies? As a first cut, the answer to this question must undoubtedly be "yes," for the simple reason that increased military expenditures on the part of *candidate great powers* could forebode consequential alterations in the global balances of power. This conclusion, however, applies most strongly to those countries that have the obvious potential to become significant powers in international politics. The "size" of the candidate power—which may be measured along multiple dimensions—is obviously the first variable conditioning our judgment, so that a China or an India merits greater attention than, say, a Malaysia or New Zealand. A second variable that should also be relevant is the location of the entity concerned. Rapidly growing countries that are strategically located and could use their increased national military capability to constrain American access to critical areas of the globe also merit close attention.

The conclusion that the United States ought to be concerned about the prospects of large and rapidly growing economies increasing their military expenditures is intuitively defensible as a "first cut." But a more considered response must be based on deeper judgments about why such military expenditure growth is occurring in each case. Simple quantitative evidence about rising military expenditures in a given country must be supplemented by more detailed analysis of the internal patterns of these expenditures. In particular, it is important to know how increased expenditures are ultimately being reflected in terms of force structure and operational competencies. Unfortunately, we could not quantitatively analyze the history of these variables for the five powers examined in this report, mainly because of the paucity of data. Fortunately, it should be easier to undertake such analysis in the context of prospective great powers because contemporary military expenditure data is more easily available and, even when unclear, can be supplemented by estimations based on other currently available factors.

The hypotheses identified in this report are particularly relevant for emerging powers because, given the availability of quantitative and qualitative data, it becomes possible to distinguish between them and so define judicious policy responses to each challenge of military expenditure growth. All three of the motives we hypothesize may require certain common responses at some level—such as developing equalizing or countervailing capabilities—because the military instruments created by other states represent tangible coercive assets that could be used to undercut larger American interests. But the urgency and magnitude of these responses could vary considerably depending on which motive is predominant. Military expenditure growth driven by ambition, for example, calls for countervailing strategies that heavily emphasize deterrence, whereas expenditure growth driven by fear may require responses that emphasize reassurance.

Understanding why prospective great powers are increasing the share of national resources devoted to the military is crucial for the making of sound policy. This understanding will require as fine-grained internal detail about foreign military expenditures as possible, but, more important, even these data must be contextualized by a larger understanding of the target country's political goals, the pattern of its state-society relations, and the character and competencies of its military forces. This effort will require much more involved analysis than that carried out in this study, but the latter should at least serve the purpose of, first, demonstrating that most great powers since the last century did increase their military burdens inexorably as a result of rising economic growth, and, second, that they did so for complex combinations of ambition, fear, and legitimacy—the exact mix of which unfortunately cannot be investigated quantitatively today because of, inter alia, the paucity of good and detailed historical statistics.

AVENUES FOR FUTURE RESEARCH

Given the limited data presented in this report, it is difficult to tell which of the hypotheses actually explain why states devote more resources to their respective militaries. In this section we discuss some avenues for future research. Specifically, we suggest what kind of evidence might help us determine which hypotheses are more helpful in understanding the behavior of states experiencing rapid economic growth. Below, we present the individual components of each hypothesis and sketch the evidence that might confirm the causal logic of the hypotheses in either a statistical or case study analysis.

The Ambition Hypothesis

The ambition hypothesis contends that states experiencing economic growth accumulate greater foreign ambitions that motivate them to increase their military expenditures. The relevant variables for testing this hypothesis include measures of economic growth, government centralization, ability to tax, and aggressive foreign policies.

Economic growth. A state's economic wealth represents the first part of the causal chain of the ambition hypothesis. Indicators for this variable are readily available. In this report we measure economic well-being by examining two different measures of a state's industrial capacity. When possible, we use a state's gross domestic product. For states like Russia where accurate estimates of GDP seem unreliable, energy consumption as well as iron and steel production are used as measures of economic growth.

Centralization. By centralization, we refer to whether states possess a highly centralized policymaking authority. It seems reasonable to construct a scale to measure the degree of centralization in a state's form of government. For example, tsarist Russia represents a state with a highly centralized government. All of the state's political power rested in the hands of the government in St. Petersburg. As an autocracy, the tsarist regime represents the clearest example of a centralized government. Japan would also seem to lie on this part of the scale. With its regional governments, Germany probably lies in the middle of the scale. The United States, with its federal system and representative form of government, might illustrate the most decentralized government on the scale.

Whether a government is more or less democratic does not capture the logic of centralization. In other words, centralization is not a proxy for regime type. For example, Britain in this period possessed a democratic system of government that was also highly centralized. The concept of centralization captures the notion that states with powerful central governments are better able to translate economic wealth into military power.

Extraction. States vary in their ability to transform their economic capabilities into military capabilities. Some states might experience rapid economic growth but remain incapable of marshaling that wealth for increasing government expenditures. We rely on the concept of extraction to measure the unequal variation of economic resources available to different governments. One possible way to measure extraction is to examine a state's taxation capabilities.

Aggressive foreign policies. If the ambition hypothesis is accurate, states that experience economic growth should embark on aggressive foreign policies. Two possible indicators of aggressive foreign policies exist. First, we can examine a state's diplomacy. States with expansionist foreign policies tend to practice brinksmanship diplomacy. They believe that the best way to succeed in international politics is not through cooperation but through coercion. One observable outcome of an aggressive foreign policy is the number of foreign diplomatic crises a state instigates.

Second, states with aggressive foreign policies should seek territorial expansion. Greedy states should attempt to either establish colonies or extend their spheres of influence by undertaking greater extended deterrence commitments. A cheap way of acquiring territory is by forcing weak states to become allies. For example, in the late nineteenth century, the United States consolidated its sphere of influence in the Western Hemisphere through the Monroe Doctrine. For the United States in the early part of this century, American security did not depend on dominating its weak neighbors to the south. Researchers should see greedy states expand their international commitments for the sole purpose of controlling a region. Perhaps the easiest measure of aggressive foreign policy would be to count the number of wars started against weak neighbors.

The Fear Hypothesis

The fear hypothesis argues that states will increase their military spending when they perceive heightened threats to their security. The relevant variables for testing this hypothesis are the threat indicators states consider when evaluating their security environment, including the aggregate capabilities of neighbors, national geography, the offense-defense balance, and perceptions of neighbors' intentions.

Aggregate capabilities of neighbors. The term aggregate capabilities refers to a state's economic and military power. Measurements of these capabilities are readily available. Indicators of economic capabilities include gross domestic product, energy consumption, iron and steel production, as well as population size. Ascertaining a state's military power is somewhat more difficult. However, the problem is not insurmountable. Measurements of military power might include the number of military personnel per state as well as a state's military expenditures. To control for population size, future researchers might examine per-capita military personnel.[1]

Geography. When assessing their strategic situation, states gauge whether their own geography makes conquest easy or hard. A future research project might create a scale to indicate how geography abets or diminishes a state's security. For instance, large bodies of water typically make conquest difficult. Because amphibious landings are difficult, in the past such countries as Britain and the United States possessed greater security than the great continental European powers. Germany, for example, has constantly faced the possibility of a two-front war against France and Russia. Moreover, researchers should consider using geography as an interaction term with aggregate capabilities. Put a different way, states that possess few geographic barriers to conquest and face powerful neighbors are likely to feel insecure. Again, the German case seems a good example of this type of security problem captured by such an interaction term.

Offense-defense balance. The notion of the offense-defense balance refers to how military technology affects the probability of success in warfare. When military technology makes conquest easy, offensive strategies dominate. However, finding appropriate indicators for this concept is difficult. One potential way of measuring the offense-defense balance is to perform net assessments. Research might examine whether states face neighbors capable of achieving a quick and decisive victory against them. The ratio of forces arrayed against a state can also serve as an indicator of the offense-defense balance. A force ratio of greater than three-to-one typically implies that the offense is dominant.

---

[1]For more on this issue, see Tellis et al. (2000).

Perception of a neighbor's intentions. Measuring perceptions about the intentions of neighboring states is perhaps even more difficult. One possible variable might be a measure of ideology. Presumably, neighbors with similar ideologies are more likely to establish amicable relations, while states with hostile ideologies are unlikely to be allies. For example, ideology was probably a strong factor behind the Marxist Soviet Union's inability to coordinate its security policy with capitalist Britain and France in the 1930s.

The Legitimacy Hypothesis

The legitimacy hypothesis argues that governments faced with domestic threats to their security embark on aggressive foreign policies and increase military spending to garner support at home. The relevant variables for testing this hypothesis include the threats to a regime's legitimacy, the prevalence of security myths and propaganda, and the type of governmental regime.

Threats to a regime's legitimacy. Various measures of a government's legitimacy exist. Although there is no consensus on which of these are best, we suggest a few that might make future research more fruitful. One possible measure of a state's legitimacy might stem from public opinion polls. The problem with this approach is that such data are not available for the period we examined. Another approach involves an examination of the level of political violence a state encounters. Evidence for "illegitimate" regimes include the frequency of assassination attempts, worker strikes, or revolutions. This information could be compiled as an index measuring political instability.

Security myths and propaganda. Security myths are used by governments to justify aggressive foreign policies. They are employed by insecure regimes to convince their political constituents that security threats exist—and that only expansionist foreign policy will improve the country's strategic situation. One measure of the use of security myths would involve looking at civil-military relations. Past research suggests that societies with militaries lacking civilian oversight are more susceptible to security myths. Researchers might produce a dummy variable to account for states with poor civil-military relations.

Regime type. This concept refers to the type of government a state possesses, in particular whether it is democratic or authoritarian. In general, the less democratic a state's government, the greater the probability that it will react to concerns about its legitimacy by pursuing an expansionist foreign policy. Democratic governments find it more difficult to propagate security myths or other forms of propaganda.

Because of the numerous political histories available, researchers should find it easy to code the types of governments states possesses over time. Again, adding a simple dummy variable to control for undemocratic states might serve as an adequate research strategy.

What steps should future research take? First, we need to examine the causal mechanism of each hypothesis more closely. The case studies used here only sought to determine if correlations existed between the factors identified in each hypothesis and the dependent variable, military spending. A better use of case studies might be to test the causal mechanism through process tracing.[2] Such an analysis asks whether policymakers (or any other relevant actors) behave and think in the ways our hypotheses predict. These questions point to the unique predictions made by each hypothesis. Process tracing offers the researcher the opportunity to test these unique predictions of a hypothesis and differentiate among alternative explanations. To process trace, a future study would need to conduct, at the very least, a survey of the secondary historical research for each case or examine primary source materials.

Second, another possible step involves a more systematic test of the hypotheses. While case studies are best at testing a causal mechanism, statistical methods are best at testing the background conditions of a hypothesis and determining the independent effects of its individual variables. An ideal research design would include case studies as well as statistical analyses. The problem facing statistical methods in this study is that operationalizing the variables in the three hypotheses is difficult. In other words, we need better measures or indicators of the variables that we suggest may explain military spending.

---

[2]On process tracing, see the explanation provided by Van Evera (1997). For the first discussion of process tracing, see George and McKeown (1985, pp. 21–58.)

Lastly, the case studies suggest that our analysis probably overlooked some important features of a state's domestic politics. The legitimacy hypothesis posited only one possible way in which internal political struggles might influence a government's decision about military spending. Given the lack of explanatory power offered by the legitimacy hypothesis in our first-cut case studies, a better approach might consider testing for variation by looking at a state's political institutions.

BIBLIOGRAPHY

Adamthwaite, Anthony, *France and the Coming of the Second World War, 1936–1939,* London: Cass, 1977.

Art, Robert, "A Defensible Defense: American's Grand Strategy After the Cold War," *International Security,* Vol. 15, No. 4, Spring 1991, pp. 5–53.

Babin, Nehama Ella, "The Impact of Military Expenditures on Economic Growth and Development in the Less Developed Countries," Ph.D. Dissertation, College Park, MD: University of Maryland, 1986.

Ball, Nicole, "Defense and Development: A Critique of the Benoit Study," *Economic Development and Cultural Change,* Vol. 31, No. 3, 1983, pp. 507–524.

Bairoch, P., "International Industrialization Levels from 1750 to 1980," *Journal of European Economic History,* Vol. 11, No. 2, Spring 1982.

Barnhart, Michael A., "Japanese Economic Security and the Origins of the Pacific War," *Journal of Strategic Studies,* Vol. 4, No. 2, 1981, pp. 105–124.

Barnhart, Michael A., *Japan Prepares for Total War: The Search for Economic Security, 1919–1941,* Ithaca, NY: Cornell University Press, 1987.

Beale, Howard K., *Theodore Roosevelt and the Rise of America to World Power,* New York: Collier Books, 1962.

Beasley, W.G., *Japanese Imperialism, 1894–1945,* Oxford: Oxford University Press, 1987.

Beasley, W.G., *The Meiji Restoration,* Stanford, CA: Stanford University Press, 1972.

Bell, P.M.H., *The Origins of the Second World War in Europe,* London: Longman, 1986.

Bemis, Samuel Flagg, *The Latin American Policy of the United States,* New York: Harcourt, Brace, and Company, 1943.

Benoit, Emile, *Defense and Economic Growth in Developing Countries,* Lexington, MA: Lexington Books, D.C. Heath and Company, 1973.

Benoit, Emile, "The Monetary and Real Costs of National Defense," *American Economic Review,* Vol. 58, No. 2, May 1968, pp. 398–416.

Blake, Nelson, "Background of Cleveland's Venezuela Policy," *American Historical Review,* Vol. 47, No. 2, January 1942, pp. 259–276.

Bridge, F.R. and Roger Bullen, *The Great Powers and the European State System, 1815–1914,* New York: Longman, 1980.

Brunschwig, Henri, *French Colonialism, 1871–1914: Myths and Realities,* London: Pall Mall Press, 1964.

Calleo, David, *The German Problem Reconsidered: Germany and the World Order, 1870 to the Present,* Cambridge, UK: Cambridge University Press, 1978.

Carr, E.H., *The Bolshevik Revolution, 1917–1923,* New York: Macmillan, 1953.

Castillo, Jasen J., *The Will to Win: The Societal Origins of Military Power,* Ph.D. dissertation, The University of Chicago, forthcoming.

Chan, Steve, "Grasping the Peace Dividend: Some Propositions on the Conversion of Swords into Plowshares," *Mershon International Studies Review,* Vol. 39, 1995, pp. 53–95.

Chowdhury, Abdur R, "A Causal Analysis of Defense Spending and Economic Growth," *Journal of Conflict Resolution,* Vol. 35, No. 1, March 1991, pp. 80–97.

Crankshaw, Edward, *In the Shadow of the Winter Palace: Russia's Drift Towards Revolution, 1825–1917,* New York: Viking Press, 1976.

Crowley, James, *Japan's Quest for Autonomy,* Princeton, NJ: Princeton University Press, 1966.

Dalleck, Robert, *Franklin D. Roosevelt and American Foreign Policy, 1932–1945,* Oxford: Oxford University Press, 1979.

de Grunwald, Constantine, *Tsar Nicholas I,* Blight Patmore (trans.), London: Futura Publications, 1954.

Drummond, Donald Francis, *The Passing of American Neutrality, 1937–1941,* New York: Greenwood Press, 1968.

Duus, Peter, *The Rise of Modern Japan,* Boston: Houghton Mifflin, 1976.

Erickson, John, *The Soviet High Command: A Military-Political History, 1918–1941,* New York: St. Martin's Press, 1962.

Fair, Raymond C., "The Estimation of Simultaneous Equation Models with Lagged Endogenous Variables and First Order Serially Correlated Errors," *Econometrica,* May 1970.

Fischer, Fritz, *World Power or Decline: The Controversy over Germany's Aims in the First World War,* Lancelot Farrar, Robert Kimber, and Rita Kimber (trans.), New York: W.W. Norton, 1974.

Fischer, *War of Illusions, German Policies from 1911 to 1914,* Marian Jackson (trans.), New York: W.W. Norton, 1975.

Flora, Peter, et al., *State, Economy, and Society in Western Europe 1815–1975: A Data Handbook in Two Volumes,* Chicago: St. James Press, 1987.

Geiss, Immanuel, *German Foreign Policy,* London: Routledge and Keegan, 1976.

Gellner, Ernest, *Nations and Nationalism,* Ithaca, NY: Cornell University Press, 1983.

George, Alexander L., and Timothy McKeown, "Case Studies and Theories of Organizational Decision Making," in *Advances in Information Processing in Organizations,* Greenwich, CT: JAI Press, 1985.

Gerschenkron, Alexander, *Economic Backwardness in Historical Perspective: a Book of Essays,* Cambridge, MA: Harvard University Press, 1962.

Gilpin, Robert, *War and Change in World Politics,* Cambridge: Cambridge University Press, 1981.

Glaser, Charles L., and Chaim Kaufmann, "What Is the Offense-Defense Balance and How Can We Measure It?" *International Security,* Vol. 22, No. 4, Spring 1998, pp. 44–82.

Glaser, Charles, "Realists as Optimists: Cooperation as Self-Help," *International Security,* Vol. 19, No. 3, Winter 1994/95, pp. 50–90.

Glaser, Charles, "The Security Dilemma Revisited," *World Politics,* Vol. 50, No. 1, October 1997.

Gooch, John, *Armies in Europe,* London: Routledge and Keegan Paul, 1980.

Granger, C.W.J., "Causality, Cointegration, and Control," *Journal of Economic Dynamics and Control,* Vol. 12, 1988, pp. 551–560.

Granger, C.W.J., "Investigating Causal Relations by Econometric Models and Cross-Spectral Methods," *Econometrica,* Vol. 37, August 1969, pp. 424–438.

Grossman, P., "Industrialization in of Russia and the Soviet Union," in Carlo Cipolla (ed.), *Fontanar Economic History of Europe,* Vol. 4, Part 2, Hassocks, England: Harvester Press, 1976–1977.

Gurr, Ted Robert, Keith Jaggers, and Will Moore, "The Transformation of the Western State: The Growth of Democracy, Autocracy, and State Power Since 1800," *Studies in Comparative International Development,* Vol. 25, No. 1, 1990, pp. 73–108.

Haslam, Jonathan, *The Soviet Union and the Struggle for Collective Security in Europe, 1933–1939,* New York: St. Martin's Press, 1984.

Heinrichs, Waldo, *Threshold of War: Franklin Delano Roosevelt and American Entry into World War II,* Oxford: Oxford University Press, 1988.

Herrmann, David G., *The Arming of Europe and the Making of the First World War,* Princeton, NJ: Princeton University Press, 1996.

Hildebrand, George, "Defense Expenditures and the Problem of Deflation," *American Economic Review,* Vol. 44, Issue 2, May 1954, pp. 410–422.

Hildreth, G., and J.Y. Lu, "Demand Relations with Autocorrelated Disturbances," *Michigan State University Agricultural Experiment Station, Technical Bulletin 276,* November 1960.

Hochmann, *The Soviet Union and the Failure of Collective Security, 1934–1938,* Ithaca, NY: Cornell University Press, 1984.

Howard, Michael, "Men Against Fire: Expectations of War in 1914," *International Security,* Vol. 9, No. 1, Summer 1984, pp. 41–57.

Howard, Michael, *War in European History,* London: Oxford University Press, 1976.

Hsiao, C., "Causality Tests in Econometrics," *Journal of Economic Dynamics and Control,* Vol. 2, 1979, pp. 321–346.

Hsiao, C., "Autoregressive Modeling and Money Income Causality Detection," *Journal of Monetary Economics,* Vol. 7, No. 1, 1981, pp. 85–106.

Hull, Isabel V., *The Entourage of Kaiser Wilhelm II, 1888–1918,* Cambridge: Cambridge University Press, 1982.

Huntington, Samuel P., "Why International Primacy Matters," *International Security,* Vol. 17, No. 4, Spring 1993, pp. 68–83.

Japan Statistical Association (JSA), *Historical Statistics of Japan,* Tokyo: Statistics Bureau, Management and Coordination Agency, 1987.

Jarausch, Konrad, *The Enigmatic Chancellor: Betmann Hollweg and the Hubris of Imperial Germany,* New Haven: Yale University Press, 1973.

Jelavich, Barbara, *St. Petersburg and Moscow, Tsarist and Soviet Foreign Policy, 1814–1974,* Bloomington, IN: Indiana University Press, 1974.

Jensen, Marius, "Japanese Imperialism: Late Meiji Perspectives," in Ramon Myers and Mark Pettie (eds.), *The Japanese Colonial Empire, 1895–1945*, Princeton, NJ: Princeton University Press, 1984.

Jervis, Robert, "Cooperation Under the Security Dilemma," *World Politics,* Vol. 30, No. 2, 1978.

Jervis, Robert, *Perception and Misperception in International Politics,* Princeton, NJ: Princeton University Press, 1976.

Jervis, Robert, *The Logic of Images in International Relations,* Princeton, NJ: Princeton University Press, 1970.

Joerding, Wayne, "Economic Growth and Defense Spending. Granger Causality," *Journal of Development Economics,* Vol. 21, 1986, pp. 35–40.

Johansen, Søren, "Statistical Analysis of Cointegration Vectors," *Journal of Economic Dynamics and Control,* Vol. 12, 1988, pp. 231–254.

Joll, James, *The Origins of the First World War,* London: Longman, 1984.

Jones, Sean-Lynn, "Offense-Defense Theory and Its Critics," *Security Studies,* Vol. 4, No. 4, Summer 1995, pp. 660–691.

Kaiser, David E., "Germany and the Origins of the First World War," *Journal of Modern History,* Vol. 55, September 1983, pp. 442–474.

Kaiser, David E., *Economic Diplomacy and the Origins of World War II,* Princeton, NJ: Princeton University Press, 1980.

Kemp, Tom, *Industrialization in Nineteenth Century Europe,* London: Longman, 1969.

Kennedy, Paul, "The First World War and the International Power System," *International Security,* Vol. 9, No. 1, Summer 1984, pp. 7–40.

Kennedy, Paul, *The Rise and Fall of the Great Powers,* New York: Vintage Books, 1987.

Keylor, William R., *The Twentieth-Century World: An International History,* New York: Oxford University Press, 1984.

Knight, Malcolm, Norman Loayza, and Delano Villanueva, "The Peace Dividend: Military Spending Cuts and Economic Growth," *IMF Staff Papers,* Vol. 43, No. 1, 1996, pp. 1–37.

Kobayashi, Ushisaburo, *Military Industries of Japan,* Oxford: Oxford University Press, 1922.

Organski, A.F.K., and Jacek Kugler, *The War Ledger,* Chicago: University of Chicago Press, 1980.

Kupchan, Charles, *The Vulnerability of Empire,* Ithaca, NY: Cornell University Press, 1994.

Kusi, Newman Kwado, "Economic Growth and Defense Spending in Developing Countries. A Causal Analysis," *Journal of Conflict Resolution,* Vol. 38, No. 1, March 1994, pp. 152–159.

Lafeber, Walter, "The 'Lion in the Path': The U.S. Emergence as a World Power," *Political Science Quarterly,* Vol. 101, No. 5, 1986, pp. 705–718.

Leontief, Wassily, et al., "The Economic Impact—Industrial and Regional—of an Arms Cut," *Review of Economics and Statistics,* Vol. 47, Issue 3, August 1965, pp. 217–241.

Lippmann, Walter, "Security, Not Sentiment," in Herbert J. Bass (ed.), *America's Entry into World War I,* New York: Holt, Rinehart and Winston, 1964.

Looney, Robert, "Military Keynesianism in the Third World: An Assessment of Non-Military Motivations for Arms Production," *Journal of Political and Military Sociology,* Vol. 17, Spring 1989, pp. 43–64.

Looney, Robert, *The Economics of Third World Defense Expenditures,* Contemporary Studies in Economic and Financial Analysis Series, Vol. 72, Greenwich, CT.: JAI Press, 1994.

Looney, Robert, "Arms Races in the Middle East: A Test of Causality," *Arms Control,* Vol. 2, No. 2, September 1990, pp. 179–190.

Mayer, Arno, "Domestic Causes of the First World War," in Leonard Krieger and Fritz Stern (eds.), *The Responsibility of Power,* Garden City, NY: Doubleday, 1967.

Mearsheimer, John, "Back to the Future: Instability in Europe After the Cold War," *International Security,* Vol. 15, No. 1, Summer 1990, pp. 5–56.

Mearsheimer, John, "The False Promise of International Institutions," *International Security,* Vol. 19, No. 3, Winter 1994/95, pp. 5–49.

Mitchell, Brian R., *British Historical Statistics 1750–1970,* Cambridge: Cambridge University Press, 1988.

Mitchell, Brian R., *International Historical Statistics: Europe 1750–1988,* 3rd ed., New York: Stockton Press, 1992.

Mommsen, Wolfgang, "Domestic Factors in German Foreign Policy Before 1914," *Central European History,* Vol. 6, No. 1, March 1973, pp. 11–43.

Morgenthau, Hans J., *Politics Among Nations: The Struggle for Power and Peace,* 5th ed., rev., New York: Alfred A. Knopf, 1978.

Nelson, Richard R., "The Impact of Arms Reduction of Research and Development," *American Economic Review,* Vol. 53, Issue 2, May 1963, pp. 435–446.

Pagan, Adrian R., and A.D. Hall, "Diagnostic Tests as Residual Analysis," *Econometric Reviews,* Vol. 2, No. 2, 1983, pp. 159–218.

Patrick, Hugh, "The Economic Muddle of the 1920s," in James Morley (ed.), *Dilemmas of Growth in Prewar Japan,* Princeton, NJ: Princeton University Press, 1971.

Perkins, Dexter, *The Monroe Doctrine, 1867–1907,* Baltimore: Johns Hopkins University Press, 1937.

Porch, Douglas, *The March to the Marne: The French Army, 1871–1914,* Cambridge: Cambridge University Press, 1981.

Quester, George, *Offense and Defense in the International System,* New York: J. Wiley, 1977.

Rich, Norman, *Great Power Diplomacy, 1814–1914,* Boston: McGraw Hill, 1992.

Richardson, L.F., *Arms and Insecurity,* Chicago: Quadrangle Press, 1960.

Ritter, Gerhard, *The Sword and the Scepter, the Problem of Militarism in Germany,* vol. 2, Heinz Norden (trans.), Coral Gables, FL.: University of Miami Press, 1973.

Rohl, J.C.G., *Germany Without Bismarck: The Crisis of Government in the Second Reich, 1890–1900,* Berkeley: University of California Press, 1967.

Romer, Christina D., "The Pre-War Business Cycle Reconsidered: New Estimates of Gross National Product, 1869–1908," *Journal of Political Economy,* Vol. 97, No. 1, 1989.

Ross, Graham, *The Great Powers and the Decline of the European States System, 1914–1945,* London: Longman, 1983.

Rostow, Walter W., *Stages of Economic Growth: A Non-Communist Manifesto,* Cambridge, UK: Cambridge University Press, 1960.

Sagan, Scott, "The Origins of the Pacific War," in Robert J. Rothberg and Theodore K. Rabb (eds.), *The Origins and Prevention of Major Wars,* Cambridge: Cambridge University Press, 1988.

Saunders, David, *Russia in the Age of Reform and Reaction, 1801–1881,* New York: Longman, 1992.

Schweller, Randal L., *Deadly Imbalances: Tripolarity and Hitler's Strategy of World Conquest,* New York: Columbia University Press, 1998.

Seager, Robert, "Ten Years Before Mahan: The Unofficial Case for the New Navy, 1880–1890," *Mississippi Valley Historical Review,* Vol. 40, No. 3, December 1953, pp. 501–504.

Simmel, Georg, *Conflict and the Web of Group Affiliation,* Kurt H. Wolff and Rhinehard Bendix (trans.), New York: The Free Press, 1955.

Singer, J. David, and Melvin Small, *National Material Capabilities Data, 1816–1985* [computer file], J. David Singer, University of Michigan, and Melvin Small, Wayne State University [producers], Inter-university Consortium for Political and Social Research [distributor], 1993.

Smith, Daniel J., *The Great Departure: the United States and World War One, 1914–1920,* New York: J. Wiley, 1965.

Smith, R.P., "Models of Military Expenditure," *Journal of Applied Econometrics,* Vol. 4, 1989, pp. 345–359.

Snyder, Jack L., *Myths of Empire: Domestic Politics and International Ambition,* Ithaca, NY: Cornell University Press, 1991.

Spengler, Joseph J., "Population: Notes on France's Response to Her Declining Rate of Demographic Growth," *Journal of Economic History,* Vol. 11, No. 4, Autumn 1951, pp. 403–416.

Sprout, Harold, and Margret Sprout, *The Rise of American Naval Power,* Princeton, NJ: Princeton University Press, 1939.

Spykman, Nicholas, *America's Strategy in World Politics: The United States and the Balance of Power,* New York: Harcourt, Brace, and Company, 1942.

Stoakes, Geoffrey, *Hitler and the Quest for World Dominion,* Leamington Spa, UK: Berg, 1986.

Stone, Norman, *Eastern Front, 1914–1917,* New York: Scribner's, 1975.

Taylor, A.J.P., *Bismarck: The Man and the Statesman,* New York: Vintage Books, 1967.

Taylor, A.J.P., *The Origins of the Second World War,* Greenwich, CT: Fawcett Publications, 1963.

Taylor, A.J.P., *The Struggle for Mastery in Europe, 1848–1918,* Oxford: Clarendon Press, 1954.

Tellis, Ashley J., *The Drive to Domination: Towards a Pure Realist Theory of Politics,* unpublished Ph.D. dissertation, The University of Chicago, 1994.

Tellis, Ashley J., Janice Bially, Christopher Layne, and Melissa McPherson, *Measuring National Power in the Postindustrial Age,* Santa Monica, CA: RAND, MR-1110-A, 2000.

Thorn, R.S., *The Evolution of Public Finances During Economic Development,* The Manchester School of Economic and Social Studies. 1967.

Ulam, Adam, *Expansion and Coexistence: Soviet Foreign Policy, 1917–1973,* New York: Praeger, 1974.

U.S. Bureau of the Census (Census), *Historical Statistics of the United States, Colonial Times to 1970,* Bicentennial Edition, Part 2, Washington, D.C.: U.S. Government Printing Office, 1975.

Van Evera, Stephen, "Offense, Defense and the Causes of War," *International Security,* Vol. 22, No. 4, Spring 1998, pp. 5–43.

Van Evera, Stephen, "The Cult of the Offensive and the Origins of the First World War," *International Security,* Vol. 9, No. 1, Summer 1984a, pp. 58–107.

Van Evera, Stephen, "Cause of War," Ph.D. Dissertation, Berkeley: University of California, 1984b.

Van Evera, Stephen, *Guide to Methods for Students of Political Science,* Ithaca, NY: Cornell University Press, 1997.

Vatter, Harold G., *The Drive to Industrial Maturity: The U.S. Economy, 1860–1914,* New York: Greenwood Press, 1975.

von Eyck, Erich, *Bismarck and the German Empire,* New York: Norton, 1958.

Walt, Stephen M., *Revolutions and War,* Ithaca, NY: Cornell University Press, 1995.

Walt, Stephen M., *The Origins of Alliances,* Ithaca, NY: Cornell University Press, 1987.

Waltz, Kenneth N., *Theory of International Politics,* Reading, MA.: Addison-Wesley, 1979.

Weinberg, Gerhard, *The Foreign Policy of Hitler's Germany; Diplomatic Revolution in Europe, 1933–36,* Chicago: University of Chicago Press, 1970.

Wendt, Alexander, *Social Theory of International Politics,* Cambridge: Cambridge University Press, 1999.

Wernette, J. Philip, "Financing the Defense Program," *American Economic Review,* Vol. 31, Issue 4, December 1941, pp. 754–766.

Wolf, Charles Jr., "Economic Success, Stability, and the 'Old' International Order," *International Security,* Vol. 6, No. 1, Summer 1981, pp. 75–92.

Wolfson, Murray, and Homa Shabahang, "Economic Causation in the Breakdown of Military Equilibrium," *Journal of Conflict Resolution,* Vol. 35, No. 1, March 1991, pp. 43–67.

Zakaria, Fareed, "Realism and Domestic Politics," *International Security,* Vol. 17, No. 1, Summer 1992, pp. 1771–1798.

Zakaria, Fareed, *From Wealth to Power: The Unusual Origins of America's World Role,* Princeton, NJ: Princeton University Press, 1998.

Zycher, Benjamin, and Tad Daley, *Military Dimensions of Communist Systems,* Santa Monica, CA: RAND, R-3593-USDP, 1988.